I Was
Made for More

I Was
Made for More

Bobbi Reed

PUBLISHING
& associates

COPYRIGHT

Unless otherwise indicated, all Scripture quotations are taken from the New King James Version of the Bible, copyright © 1979, 1980, 1982, Thomas Nelson, Inc., Publishers. All Scripture quotations marked KJV are taken from the King James Version of the Bible.

I Was Made for More

ISBN: 978-1-944566-64-7

Copyright ©2024 Robin Reed

Bush Publishing & Associates, LLC books may be ordered everywhere books are sold, Amazon.com and B&N.com

For further information, please contact:
Bush Publishing & Associates, Tulsa, Oklahoma
info@BushPublishing.com
Visit us at: www.bushpublishing.com

Printed in the United States of America.

No portion of this book may be used or reproduced by any means: graphic, electronic or mechanical, including photocopying, recording, taping, or by any information storage retrieval system, without the written permission of the publisher, except in the case of brief quotations embodied in critical articles and reviews.

Disclaimer: Names in the book have been changed to protect as much privacy as possible and still be able to have others understand life's challenges.

Table of Contents

Introduction ix

Chapter One
Early Childhood Memories 1

Chapter Two
My Teenage Years 14

Chapter Three
My Father 35

Chapter Four
My Abusive Marriage 43

Chapter Five
Post-Abortion Syndrome 65

Chapter Six
Music Is in My Blood 69

Chapter Seven
Single Parenting 81

Chapter Eight
Sexual Addiction 92

Chapter Nine
The Consequences and Behaviors of Abuse 101

Chapter Ten
My Military Life 109

Chapter Eleven
Sexual Trauma and PTSD 114

Chapter Twelve
Breaking Up Is Hard To Do 118

Chapter Thirteen
Dating After Divorce 130

Chapter Fourteen
My Christian Walk. 137

Chapter Fifteen
My Heritage 153

Chapter Sixteen
Never Give Up Hope 163

Chapter Seventeen
My Children Today 174

Chapter Eighteen
Where My Life is Now 185

Introduction

It is with the Holy Spirit in my heart along with the Word that I write this introduction to my journey!

The purpose of this book is to help others. Many years ago, at about the age of 32, I received a word from God. He told me that all of the pain, hurts, and challenges that I have survived and continue to grow from, would one day be used to help other women. This word was hidden in my heart for many years as I continued to grow, be molded, and endure new challenges in my life.

Well, here we are and I am finally starting to write this book. Let me start by saying that everyone has a story to tell. I am not special because I have survived all that I have. I am not special because many women have survived similar challenges. I am not special because I am writing this book. I was called by my Lord to do this and am choosing to heed that call. All of our callings and ministries are chosen individually for us. We just have to obey them. When we don't obey them, we bring new challenges into our lives. It certainly is not easy to obey God and His will for us at times, but when we do the paths are definitely smoother.

I have been blocked from writing this book for several years. I did not understand it at the time, but as always, God's timing is best. I fully believe that I had more growing to do along with more grieving about my past. We are never done and never perfect; always a work in progress.

I remain daily open to God's correction, growth, and His will. As I start to write this book, I am headed to a three-day women's conference. I attended the same conference about four years ago and it helped me to dig deep to remove some of my pain and to heal my heart more. If you have any opportunity to participate in conferences such as these, do so. Along with counseling, prayer, and fasting, these are necessary steps to move you through challenges, for God to help you grieve your losses, along with removing roots/strongholds that are very deep.

I must say that even now, it is painful to revisit and continue to contemplate the past. While I am fully aware that it makes me who I am today – compassionate, understanding of pain, merciful and forgiving, loving, accepting of differences, and leaning on God more and more – it still can be painful. I have grown so much over the years, that I now realize that EVERY challenge, pain, rejection, loss, abuse, and my low self-esteem have given me a story to tell to help others. God blesses us in our "mess," and we also learn to lean on Him much more when things are going rough for us. After all, there is not a "TESTIMONY" without a "TEST."

I am a very open person; honest and forthright with information and feelings. I talk a lot and it has been said that I could "talk the horns off of a bull!" I hope that some of why I talk so much is because I have a lot to say – words that will help others. I know that I do talk a lot and I have always said that since my dad was a minister and my mother a teacher, I "earned my big mouth honestly." I have always believed in talking out things rather than keeping them in. If I have a conflict with someone, I am a firm believer in communication and understanding the other person first. I fully realize that there are times when words are not enough or not needed and at those times, I try hard to listen.

I have a big heart and love sharing it. While many people in my past say that I can appear rough and non-caring, those who know me, understand that I will give you my last dime if you are in need. I constantly "sow" into others' lives and believe we are here to help each other. God has placed people in my path to help me and for me to help. I have needed a lot of help through the years, especially having to raise four children pretty much by myself for more than 30 years. I was proud for many years and did not want to ask for help, but God taught me that I had to be humble. I was taking other people's blessings that they were receiving from helping me if I did not accept their help! In turn, there have been many opportunities that I have been given to help others, and it has always really blessed me to do so.

It is with this openness, honesty, and transparency that I write this book. This book is NOT intended to hurt anyone or to put anyone's business out in the public eye, except my own! There will be things that will be said that even some of those closest to me do not know. I feel that to truly help others in the manner that God wants me to, I have to be painfully honest and open about the good, bad, and ugly about myself. This will be and already is deeply painful for me. I am willing, though, to dig as deep as I have to go and to be as candid as possible to help someone else. I will not, in most cases, go into real detail. I will only let you know enough of what happened so that you can get a gist of what transpired, how I survived and grew from it, and that I am an 'expert' in the areas where I am trying to help others.

As stated earlier, the purpose is to show others that no matter what the challenges are in our lives, we are meant to make it through them and not go around them. They are meant to teach us lessons, the least of which is that God is always there WITH us through everything -even in our sins. We are not meant to stay in these challenges, but to work through them and get to the other side! This book is about not just surviving these challenges, but about being a better person because of them. It is also about how our lives are interwoven and how God places people in our lives at strategic times to teach us and continue to grow us into all that He would have us to be.

This story that I received in an email the other day from an unknown author sums up what I want you to understand about life, and why I want to encourage you no matter what stage you are in your life or what challenges you have survived. We are never finished growing and everything in our lives will continue to be a product of what has happened. We can change the type of product that we are, by submitting our hurts and pain to God for Him to heal. It also, in times of struggle, is much better to reach out to others in need, because it makes our pain seem less as we help others. It helps us take our minds off of it for a bit, and when we come back to it, it doesn't seem as large. Here is the story I received:

Quilt of Holes

As I faced my Maker at the last judgment, I knelt before the Lord along with all the other souls.

Before each of us, laid our lives, like the squares of a quilt in many piles. An angel sat before each of us sewing our quilt squares together into a tapestry that was our life.

As my angel took each piece of cloth off the pile, I noticed how ragged and empty some of my squares were. They were filled with giant holes. Each square was labeled with a part of my life that had been difficult, the challenges and temptations I was faced with in everyday life. I saw hardships that I endured, which were the largest holes of all.

I glanced around me. Nobody else had such squares. Other than a tiny hole here and there, the other tapestries were filled with rich color and the bright hues of worldly fortune. I gazed upon my own life and was disheartened.

My angel was sewing the ragged pieces of cloth together, threadbare and empty; like binding air. Finally, the time came when each life was to be displayed, and held up to the light; the scrutiny of truth. The others arose, each in turn, holding up their tapestries. So filled, their lives had been. My angel looked upon me and nodded for me to rise.

My gaze dropped to the ground in shame. I hadn't had all the earthly fortunes. I had love in my life and laughter. There had also been trials of illness and poverty. There had been false accusations that took from me my world, as I knew it. I had to start over many times. I often struggled with the temptation to quit, only to somehow muster the strength to pick up and begin again. I spent many nights on my knees in prayer, asking for help and guidance in my life.

I had often been held up to ridicule, which I endured

painfully, each time offering it up to the Father in hopes that I would not melt within my skin beneath the judgmental gaze of those who unfairly judged me.

And now, I had to face the truth. My life was what it was, and I had to accept it for what it was. I rose and slowly lifted the combined squares of my life to the light. An awe-filled gasp filled the air. I gazed around at the others who stared at me with wide eyes.

Then, I looked upon the tapestry before me. Light flooded the many holes, creating an image of the face of Christ. Then our Lord stood before me, with warmth and love in His eyes. He said, 'Every time you gave over your life to Me, it became My life, My hardships, and My struggles. Each point of light in your life is where you stepped aside and let Me shine through, until there was more of Me than there was of you.'

May all our quilts be threadbare and worn, allowing Christ to shine through!

God determines who walks into your life and it's up to you to decide who you let walk away, who you let stay, and who you refuse to let go.

This book is about my journey. These memories are written as I remember them and things as I remember them being told to me. While this book is about my journey, there were others in my life who took that journey with me. Many of the key persons will be spoken about. I will include some things remembered by them, as they allow me to, throughout this book. Again, this book is not intended to hurt anyone, expose other people's issues, or to have any sort of vengeance against anyone.

I feel the reason I had to wait so long to write this book was mainly due to where I needed to be in my life. I started on this book in 2009 but didn't start writing the chapters until 2015. It is in the year 2024, I am writing the last few chapters, editing it, and feeling released by God that it is done. Please read this book with an open, non-judgmental mind, so that the lessons that I learned can help you to be on the "victorious" side of your challenges in life. If this book helps even just one woman, all the years of work, healing, being transparent, and writing this book will be worth it!

May God bless your comings and goings along with all the in-betweens in the journeys of your life! Lean on God and those He has put in your path, and you will get through these hard things in life. Remember, "we are made for MUCH MORE!"

Chapter One

Early Childhood Memories

My earliest memory was when I was about two years old and living in Pinepoint, Maine. I knew I had a younger sister, an older brother, and two older sisters. I remember some things about the house itself, but my memories are mainly about the outdoors around my house. We would always find frogs in the birdbath and across the street were clusters of blackberry bushes. We ate many berries straight off of those bushes. Down at the dead end of the street was an elderly woman, who we (as kids) thought was a witch. We were scared of her, but I do not remember why. Another memory that sticks out to me was the time I got very upset at my sister who was just a year and a half older than me—Bonnie. I was so upset by something she did that I threw a very large rock at her and hit her in the head. It was a horrible thing to do and I felt very bad later on, as I did hurt her. I don't think I was trying to aim for her head at the time, but it did hit her head and took a decent chunk out of it. Since I was about three, I was surprised that I actually could throw a rock that hard and really hurt someone. Needless to say, I got in plenty of trouble.

Most of my early memories were of fun and interesting things. I do not remember if I was physically abused in the first ten years of my life. I do have a few pictures of me as a child. One was when I was three; I seemed carefree, happy and did not have pain in my eyes. The next one is at nine years old. I was standing with my family in a church with a man named Dr. English. He was a friend of my father's and later I learned that he had baptized all of us as kids. When I looked at this picture from the past, I saw a girl who had lost her smile and had very sad eyes. While studying for my teacher certification for Colorado many years ago, I learned that what makes a child—their character, morals, and how they see life—is formed by what happens to them in their first ten years of life. This can be changed in the years after ten, but it is usually through life-altering events.

I remember playing a lot as a young child and getting along with my siblings most of the time. When I was four years old, almost five, my father moved us to Bay Shore, New York. We lived in the Parsonage: a home that belonged to the church and was located right next to it. It was a large home, and it was well-suited for us since now there were six children in total. My dad spent a lot of time in the church office next door as well as visiting the parishioners. He took his job as a minister very seriously.

My dad always drove older Cadillacs. He could not afford a new one, so he bought them used and held onto them for as long as he could. I am not sure if it was an image thing with him—was a large car befitting of being a minister? Back in that day, there were mostly large cars anyway. Now that I think of it, it might just have been necessary for our large family. He tried to take us on outings many times throughout the years, but I am sure we were not the best-behaved children. We were close in age and had a lot of energy. There was a lot of normal sibling rivalry.

My earliest memory from the time that we moved there was attending kindergarten. As you will soon learn about me, I am an outgoing and talkative person. I believe that in order to be heard growing up in a large family, you learn to speak out frequently and loudly. Unfortunately, my kindergarten teacher did not appreciate me being so vocal. I was in trouble with her regularly. Her punishment for me, back in the period when teachers were allowed to spank the students, was to turn me over her knee. Not only did she turn me over her knee, but when she spanked me, she exposed my ruffled panties to the whole class. I remember feeling much more embarrassed about my panties being exposed than about actually getting a "whipping." I do not remember whether I was yet being abused at home or not. I should have been embarrassed about being spanked in front of my classmates, but it seems that the memory of my panties being seen by them affected me more. It is very possible that I was being abused by then, but I truly do not remember that. I am sure anyone who has been abused in any kind of way can understand that sometimes we block out memories. Maybe that is our brain's way of protecting us.

Before I begin to speak about some of the hardships in my childhood, let me first give you some family background (as I know it). As I said earlier, my father was a minister. He was originally from Pennsylvania, as was my mother. He was ordained as an Episcopalian minister and retired at the age of 75. For the majority of his years as a minister, he was a minister in the Congregational United Church of Christ denomination. Most of the churches that he pastored were small congregations.

Before meeting and marrying my mother, he had been married. He had two sons, Jack and Peter, whom I have never met. My understanding was that there were problems in the marriage and so it lasted approximately five or six years. I was a bit shocked to find out that my mother, along with my siblings and I, were not the only family my father had. I especially could not believe that I was unaware of this information until after I graduated from high school and was headed to the army.

My father also had a few sisters, of whom I may have met once or twice. I have no understanding of why I did not see my aunts more or have a relationship with them, but I suppose it had something to do with my mom. I also did not know my grandmother or grandfather on my father's side. I believe that they lived long but died when I was very young. My mom and dad met and married when she was 19 and he was 32 years old. I believe they were happy for a few years. They waited until five years or so into the marriage to have their first child. The oldest in our family was Beth. Then came Gregory, Bonnie, myself, Claudia, and Geoffrey. There was a one-and-a-half to two years difference between all of us. So, once my mom started having children, there were six of them in approximately nine years. That was a lot to handle, especially for a mother who was an only child.

My mother grew up outside Philadelphia. Her father served in the military and was a chiropractor. His office was in the home, so the family had to be very disciplined and quiet whenever my grandfather had patients. My mother grew up believing (and still does to this day) that if you were under chiropractic care, you would rarely get sick and never have any major illness. Even as she has gotten elderly and her body naturally deteriorated, she believes that because her dad was a chiropractor, she would never have a heart attack, stroke, break any bones, etcetera. My grandmother, Ethel, was an old-fashioned woman. Everything was done just so. You were dressed for every event just so. She was always well-dressed and well-mannered. I did not know my grandfather on my mother's side; he died in 1955, the year that I was born. I have seen pictures of my grandparents on both sides.

Since my mother was an only child, I am sure that she was not used to the environment she found herself in as a mother of six. I was told by her that her parents were strict, but never heard that she was abused or that physical punishment was used in her home. As I stated earlier, I do not remember when the abuse started for us children. I believe that it was after the toddler stage of our lives. Growing up, I always felt that she loved the baby and toddler stage of her children's lives, but felt out of control as we got older.

I want to make it clear that she did not single any one of her children out—all of the six children were equally abused. My memories are mostly of my own abuse, even though I was aware of my siblings suffering abuse at the same time. I recall that my sister Bonnie did not get hit as much as the rest of us. I felt that she was my mother's "pet" and rarely got into trouble. She was very bright in school and worked hard to get A's. She did, however, "turn" on our mom at about the age of 17. She became very weary of all the restrictions that Mom had on us and wanted more freedom.

We were required, at fairly young ages, to start helping with housework. It seemed impossible to participate in any activity outside the home without first doing lots of chores. I am sure that when we were young, my mother did all the housework and cooked a lot. As far back as I can remember, though, she did not do much housework other than periodically, especially spring cleaning. When we got older, we were taught how to take the heavy blinds, soak them in the tub for a bit in bleach water, and then take them to the clothesline wrapped in a towel. It seemed many times over the years that my mother would throw out her back. She wouldn't do housework often, but when she did, she did it excessively and would end up hurting herself.

Since we were growing up in an abusive environment, we siblings argued a lot as we grew older. Some of our arguments would get physical since this is all we were being shown. We got each other in trouble often, whether it was intentional or not. There is one memory that will remain with me forever because I got injured. It happened to me when I was about nine years old. There was quite a bit of snow on the ground this particular day. It was a Sunday afternoon, and my parents were entertaining some minister friends of my dad's. My bedroom was at the front of the house on the second floor. Outside the windows that faced the front of the house was a roof that went out over our front porch. My older brother slept up on the third floor. His bedroom used to be a large attic, but they had scaled it down and used half of it to make a bedroom. He had one big window in that bedroom, and it also faced the front of the house.

On this particular day, we were all taking naps. Yes, even at the older ages, we still took naps on Sundays. Greg was playing with a string, dangling it out the window. At some point, the string fell down the roof below—right outside of my window. I don't know if he came down to my bedroom or spoke to me out of the window, but somehow he communicated to me that he wanted me to get it. Now, since I have been out on the roof outside my window a few times (doing what, I do not recall), he felt it would be alright for me to reach out and get that string for him. Now, remember I said that there was snow on the ground? There was also snow on the roof that began about six to seven inches out from the window. I opened up the window, trying to reach out to get that string without having to actually get outside of the window. It did not work.

I decided that if I held onto the window frame and got outside the window, I would then be able to reach that string. I look back and wonder just what was so important about that string, but as a nine-year-old, I guess my brother wanted me to get it so I was trying to. I stepped out of the window with my bare feet. We had our pajamas on since we were down for a nap. I used my left hand to hold onto the window frame and tried to reach that string with my right hand. I reached out and thought I was going to be able to pick it up off of the roof, but I miscalculated. Instead, one of my feet slipped on the snow and I proceeded to fall down the roof to the ground below. As I rolled down the roof, I cut my chin on the edge of the roof.

I don't remember hitting the ground. I can only imagine my little body falling off the roof and my parent's guests seeing something of consequent size going past our big picture window in the living room where they were sitting. They ran outside and saw me in the snow with blood everywhere. I do remember being lifted and being wrapped in a blanket. Next, we were in the emergency room of Southside Hospital, which was five minutes down the road. I was very upset sitting in the waiting room, being covered in blood. To make matters worse, there were some kids in the waiting room with us. They were laughing at me because I was in my pajamas! They couldn't have been laughing at the blood everywhere. I was taken back to an examining room that had a very hard metal bed. I was given some type of local sedation so that they could sew up my chin. I required about nineteen stitches. They put a big bandage on my chin and my parents were told that I could only have liquids for the next week and that I could open up my mouth halfway. I asked them, "You mean I cannot talk much?" I am sure that was more of a punishment for me than the stitches and bandages were.

I stayed home from school for a week and had food fed to me only in the form of liquids. I returned to school a week later. I rode the bus to school on occasion, but I mostly walked to my elementary school. Our bus driver, Red, was a huge character loved by all the kids. He carried a wooden paddle in his bus called the "Board of Education." He was strict but very fun. When he picked me up from the bus stop upon my return, he started laughing. I still had that large bandage on my chin. What was so humorous to him was that I could not talk that much. I received a large dosage of teasing from him that lasted until I got that bandage removed. I am very sure my teacher was happy for a break from my talkative nature.

I healed just fine and seemed to take the temporary changes in diet in stride. Needless to say, my brother got in some trouble. I guess my punishment for being out on that roof was obvious. I remember feeling humiliated by those kids in the emergency room making fun of me. Why that bothered me more than the falling down the roof, stitches, and staying home for a week from school, I do not know. I did not venture out on that roof again, now being very aware of what could happen to me.

That was the only time in my childhood that I got injured by my actions. I was an active child who did many fearless things. I climbed a lot of trees. I was also a thin child with a lot of energy. I was inquisitive, so I probably got myself into lots of situations that were dangerous. I believe it was the grace of God that sustained me from being injured many times over. Most of the kids my age in the neighborhood were boys. The only girls around to play with were my sisters. Since we didn't get along as time wore on, I preferred to play outside with the boys. I was involved in baseball, tackle football, climbing trees, and lots of bike riding to different places in town. I had some falls, cuts, and bruises, but no major injuries. I would grow up to play many sports in high school and later in life with no major injuries. The only other injuries in my childhood were from my mother.

Around the age of seven, I met a girl at our church. Her family, who had at least as many kids as we did, attended my church. We were in the same Sunday School class since we were the same age; she was only five days older than me. Being of the same personality, we clicked immediately and often tried to skip out of class at church. Due to my stressful home environment, I didn't want many friends to come over. So, I tried to get permission to visit other's houses. We would go on to be friends for about 57 years.

Since we lived in the parsonage and I was a "preacher's kid" (PK), our family was at church a lot. We were at almost every event and were also called on to help do things in the church. I remember being asked to clean the boys' bathroom and how "grossed out" I was. I was responsible for cleaning the bathrooms at our house and hated it! To this day, cleaning the bathrooms is my least favorite household chore. So not only did we get to do chores at home, but we were called on often to do things at the church as well.

A memory that stands out from my younger years was when they redid part of the church. Before they knocked down the fellowship hall, we had a small driveway with a moderate yard that contained large trees and a handmade swing. The swing hung from a large maple tree and was made of large ropes and a piece of board. I have good memories of many hours spent on that swing, feeling a few carefree moments of childhood. When I used to swing, I felt as if there were no worries and no cares in the world. Our maple trees were beautiful and huge—I truly enjoyed them. There were some all around the neighborhood also. They were especially beautiful when they would shed their leaves in the fall. After living out in the west for 31 years in Colorado, I truly miss those maple trees and all of the foliage that is indigenous to the East Coast.

My sister, Bonnie, had a great green thumb. Every year she would plant and grow tomatoes. I always thought that she would grow up to be a farmer since she had such a way of growing things. I was always amazed by what the plants would produce and how hearty the tomatoes that grew under her care were. Long Island had many farms on the north shore of the island, and many times we went to gather our strawberries at some of those farms. There were always arrays of homegrown fruit and vegetable stands along the roadsides with large and delicious fresh produce. However, it was nice to have some fresh vegetables in our own backyard.

When we moved to Bay Shore and into the parsonage, the church had a fellowship hall that was attached to the rest of the church. The hall was very old and I remember it having extremely old fixtures, especially in the bathrooms. There was a small kitchen and classrooms for us to meet in for Sunday School. The other part of the church had my father's office, the choir room, and the sanctuary. The fellowship hall was torn down to build a much-needed new one.

I watched the whole process of the wrecking ball hitting the old building. I saw it all crumble down. Then, all the old rubbish was carted away. It was a very interesting and captivating process for a young child to witness. It took many days, and since we lived in the house right next to where it was going on, we had an awesome view of it around the clock. We were also able to see the building of the new one and all of the stages that it entailed.

The building of the new fellowship hall for the church was a long process. Raising the money and being involved in all the necessary events was fun. There was one negative part of building the new building, though. To build the new hall, someone felt that it was necessary to take down most of the trees in our backyard—including the one that held our swing. I know that sounds minor to most people, but to a child who was in an unstable environment, taking one of the few things that made me feel carefree was monumental.

Our backyard, which had an oversized one-car garage, became mostly a driveway. We still had a small grass area where the clothesline was and an area to keep our dog to the left of the garage. Between the garage and the house was another small grass area where we had our picnic table and our barbeque. Many summer nights, I remember my dad cooking out and enjoying eating a good meal as a family. He would cook corn on the cob wrapped in foil on the grill along with the meat.

Our front yard was also small. We lived near the corner of two very busy streets. Since our backyard was diminished and became mostly a large driveway, I believe we ventured out and played a lot around the churchyards and buildings. We also, being young adventurous children, found many places in a three-block radius to play. There were many woods—which is what we call them back east—that had many trees and great hiding places. We considered all the areas nearby that were not private yards as our places to play.

We even thought that the many cars that traveled down Union Avenue by the church were part of our play. I am ashamed to say that we were not always well-behaved children. I recall one spring when we thought it would be great fun to make hard-packed snowballs and throw them at passing cars. There were some stairs on the side of the church that went to the basement and had bushes around them. It made for the perfect hiding place to throw snowballs at the passing cars without being seen.

Being children, we did not think of the possible consequences to our fun activity. One time when we were doing this, we threw a snowball and it went into an open window of a car. Inside the car was a pregnant woman. Since the snowball came out of nowhere and hit that woman, it almost caused her to have an accident. Like with anything in life, if you keep doing the wrong thing, God will eventually have you pay a consequence for your behavior. The couple stopped the car to come and find us. I think we thought of running, but were so shocked that someone actually stopped that we didn't run far. The couple asked to see our parents.

I think that my dad was the one at home at the time. We did not get a spanking, since my dad never hit us. I guess he figured that since mom did that so often he didn't need to add to the abuse. I do remember getting in a heap of trouble and being punished though. I think that we were not allowed to go out and play for quite a few days. This was especially hard for me since I have always been a social and adventurous type of child. Needless to say, this ended our throwing snowballs at the cars passing by the church on Union Boulevard.

In retrospect, I see now that something that happened to our family house might have been connected as another consequence of this misbehavior. One Halloween, we were out trick-or-treating as usual around the neighborhood. We came home and dumped all of our candy together. We were allowed to have one piece before we headed off to bed. When we awoke in the morning, we went outside of the house to remove some decorations.

Someone had egged our house. They probably threw about a dozen eggs that had hit the front of our house. They did not break any windows, which was surprising since we had a huge picture window in the front of the house. They did, however, hit the painted front of the house. I remember how hard the dried-up egg was to remove from the painted shingles. I guess that is a good example of "you reap what you sow." There was quite a mess and it was very hard to clean up. You could not just leave it, because the egg eats up paint, so it had to be cleaned up right away.

As stated earlier, I was a very social child. I only saw my best friend on Sundays. Her family's home was about 20 minutes away in the neighboring town of West Islip. We mostly saw each other when her family would come to church on Sundays. I had mostly male friends. There were not a lot of girls in my neighborhood, so my choices of playmates were mostly boys. I was definitely a tomboy, so that suited me just fine.

My earliest memory of a "boyfriend" was in 4th grade. Of course, at that time, there was nothing other than a crush on this boy. He lived down the street from me and he was beautiful. His mother was the most beautiful woman I had ever seen. We hung out a lot together, both in school and out of school. I am not sure if he was aware that my feelings were more than a friend should have, but I felt them.

Now that I look back at this, it does seem an awfully young age to have a crush on someone. Usually, girls who seem to have "boyfriend relationships" early in their lives do so because they are missing something from their father at home. I will talk more about my dad and what he meant to me later in this book. I did not feel that I was missing anything from my dad. If anything, my dad is the person in my life who kept me sane and somewhat normal throughout all the abuse bestowed on me by my mother.

My friend and I were friends for many years but were "boyfriend and girlfriend" for about four years. I remember during that period when we really liked each other, a very pretty girl moved to town. She was Puerto Rican like he was. I wondered if he would like her more than me because they were of the same race. I was interested in her friendship because she was nice and pretty. Unfortunately, I was not the only one that liked Mary. My "boyfriend" more than liked her as a friend, and I remember those were my first feelings of jealousy.

I grew up in a diverse environment. Most of the kids that I grew up with were non-Caucasian. My town was a fair-sized one and the kids from the neighboring village of Brightwaters also attended school with us. In that village, the population was mostly Caucasian and well-off. The population of Bay Shore was racially diverse with each race having different levels of income. No one race was "rich" or "poor." We had several elementary schools, but only one middle school and one high school.

Music was and always has been very important in my life. I sang from as young as I can remember with all of us kids singing in our church choirs. We also all played a musical instrument. At the age of nine, in third grade, we all were introduced to the tonette. Back then, all children had music classes in school and were taught how to read music. These were the times that I felt free. A love of music developed early on. When I sang or played the violin, I felt as if I was born to go forth in music and I felt safe. I would not realize until many years later that God gave me these gifts, and no matter what abuse or awful events were to happen to me, no one could quiet the music in my soul. I will discuss music and how important it was in my life in a later chapter.

I remember feeling awfully insecure at a very young age. I sucked my right thumb until I was about nine years old. I still have evidence of this, as my right thumb is larger than my left. Also, I have an overbite where my upper teeth overlap my lower ones. Due to the fact that we did not have any extra money, and there were six of us kids, I was never able to have any orthodontic work to correct this. As with many things in my life, I learned to live with it and make the best of a bad situation.

I also used to chew my nails and twist my hair. One time, when I was about six or seven, I twisted my long hair so much in one area that I had to cut that piece out. Another time, I went to bed with a piece of gum in my mouth, and when I woke up, it was stuck in my hair. That piece had to be cut out also. My hair was always pretty growing up. It was usually long and at times it grew down to my waist. I had thick hair that got darker and darker as I grew older. I remember that my hair was a source of joy to me; through these years, I felt great pleasure in wearing many different hairstyles and experimenting with barrettes, ribbons, and rubber bands.

As stated earlier, I do not remember when the abuse started. I only have a few pictures of when I was a child. The picture of when I was three seemed to be the last one where I looked happy. When I look at it, we as a family were all standing closely together. My father seemed happy, as did most of us kids. My youngest brother had not yet been born. It was taken in front of a fireplace and I believe it to be our home in Pinepoint, Maine. We did not move to Bay Shore, New York until

I was four. I see a pretty little girl with yellow-blonde ringlets, a pretty dress, and a carefree smile.

As anyone who has been in counseling knows, we all have a little girl/boy inside of us. As I look back and ask God to show me where my little girl was last happy, He shows me that picture. I was three and I had not yet felt or internalized the gross dysfunction in my home. I go back to that age and what I looked like (thanks to the picture and God's giving me the memories) and embrace her. I want to protect her from the awful things that are about to happen to her. I want to comfort her and tell her that no matter how hard it is going to get, she will be alright. She will learn through all her pain to love others. I assure her that even though she will not understand it until much later in her life, God will be with her in every tragedy and awful event. He is not only with us in the good times. With God's help, I would grow, mature, and do the work I needed to in counseling to learn from this abuse and heartache. I would later on desire to help others in similar situations. As stated in my introduction, God confirmed to me about 33 years ago that He would use my past and all of these things I survived to help other women. That is one of my strongest passions and desires today.

Chapter Two
My Teenage Years

Most of my memories of my emotional and physical abuse take place in my teenage years. I am sure there was verbal abuse also, with words that made me feel worthless being said frequently to me. The emotional abuse was not apparent to me as a child, but it is now that I am an adult. I will not go into gross detail, but I will tell you enough to show you my pain and to help you understand what God has brought me through. I do need to make sure the reader understands that I am an expert in the topics that I am discussing. The whole reason for writing this book is to help other women and men understand that no matter what happens in life, we can recover! With some counseling and hard work (along with God's healing), we can be whole again. We also can help others who are going through similar challenges!

Along with the abuse, there were memories of me as a teen having fun and doing "normal" things. I know many of my actions as a teen were because of my inner strength trying to help me cope with the ugliness in my home. I tried very hard to be absent from my home as much as possible. I was and still am a people person. I love people for all of their beauty and their faults. I enjoy interacting with others in various forms and find pleasure in seeing the different kinds of people there are. Even though we all have our own characters, looks, hurts, and pains, we all have several things in common. We have all experienced pain in diverse forms and durations. We all want to be loved and acknowledged. We all want to be accepted and have a voice of our own.

I felt strongly that I did not have a voice as I was growing up. There were so many of us kids, so we had to speak loudly and quickly to get attention from our parents. I imagine we had to interrupt quite often. I was told many times as a young girl that I had a voice that "projected" very easily. Even though I talked often and was a great communicator with others outside my home, I had no real voice within my home. I definitely could not control what was happening to me.

My dad could not control what was happening to us either. He felt very out of control as a parent because even though he loved us kids dearly, as the head of his household, he could not protect us from our mother. He tried many times and threatened her often. Back then, there was a huge stigma about divorce. In addition, the police would not stop a parent who chose to "parent" their children through abuse.

I called the police one time on my mother after a particularly harsh session of abuse. I was about 15 or 16 years old. I had had enough and felt that the police would help me. When they arrived at the house, they talked to me and my mother. They told me that as long as my mother had a roof over my head and fed me—even if it was just bread and water every day—that she was providing for me and she was not doing anything wrong. I remember feeling devastated. If the police would not help me and my father could not control it, where could I turn for validation and aid?

I ran away from home when I was 15 and 16 years old about seven times. I just could not tolerate the abuse any longer. The physical abuse was rampant along with the emotional and mental abuse. I would run to my boyfriend's home and stay overnight in his basement, unbeknownst to his parents. I would go to school the next day and then go home. There were no shelters for battered kids that I could seek refuge in back then. I felt hopeless after surviving so many years of abuse at my mother's hands. I don't know what kept me going or what never allowed me to think of killing myself. I had every reason to do so, but that thought never entered my mind. I believe that God was there with me, and even though at that time I did not have a personal relationship with the Lord, I knew that I could lean on him.

I finally stopped running away because of my dad. He knew that I felt I had no choice but to run away to survive. He finally made it clear to me that he worried so much when I was out there "in the streets" and he did not know where I was. It was about the seventh time I had fled the home and did the usual of staying over at my boyfriend's house in the basement overnight. I went to school (it is surprising that, under the circumstances, I did not skip school) the next day. While in school, I received a note from the assistant principal to report to his office. I was trying to rack my brain to figure out what I had done wrong in school to get sent to his office. When I got there, the principal was there and let me know that my dad had called up to the school. He explained that my dad had instructed them to have me there after school to pick me up. I reported back to his office after school and my dad was sitting there, waiting for me.

When we got home, my dad had a long talk with me. He let me know that while he totally understood why I was running away, I had to stop. He told me that it was very hurtful to him not to know where I was or what could be happening to me. My father never laid a hand on me in all of my years growing up, but he did that day. He proceeded to tell me that "it was going to hurt him more than me" when he spanked me. Now, we all have heard that statement many times growing up, but something made me believe him. It was probably the tears in his eyes as he took off his belt and hit me a few times on my bottom. I knew in my heart, after all the abuse my mother had done to us kids, that spanking me was the last thing he wanted to do. I do not know why he chose to do that and not something else—maybe it was a lack of knowledge or he felt that somehow, it coming from him would make a lasting impression on me. I am here today to say that it did! I never ran away again, even though the circumstances with my mother did not change. I remember what he said and the tears in his eyes and that would stop me. He also told me, before he spanked me, that he loved me very much and didn't want anything to happen to one of his precious children.

Soon after that incident, I received a pink pass from the teacher in class one day. It had a date and time after school (a few days later) to see Mr. Smith. I did know someone named Mr. Smith, but I wondered why I had to go talk to him after school. The day arrived, and I proceeded as instructed to Mr. Smith's office. I quickly learned that Mr. Smith was the school psychiatrist and had been referred to me by the principal. I guessed while talking to my dad that the principal felt I needed to talk to someone, especially since I had run away quite a few times before that last time.

Mr. Smith asked me what was going on at home. At first, I wasn't sure if I could trust him enough to tell him the awful truth. I didn't have any trouble telling my friends about it, being the outgoing child that I was. I did have trouble trusting authority figures that were not my dad, though—understandably. After a while of talking to him, I began to open up. It took several sessions, but I told him (in as much detail as I could) about all of the awful things that were happening to me. I shared with him that these acts were not only happening to me but all of my brothers and sisters as well. I don't remember that any of my siblings fought back, but I was honest with him that I had certainly started doing so. I shared with him, through many tears, the events that were taking place in my home and how I was being affected by them. I still didn't trust him fully, but I felt that just maybe, someone in authority would help me this time. The police didn't care and my dad seemed powerless to stop what was happening, but maybe this was different.

After about the third or fourth visit, my dad was asked to come see Mr. Smith. My dad talked to him without me there because Mr. Smith wanted to hear my dad's side of the story. After my dad met with Mr. Smith for about two hours, he met me after school and took me out to get pizza. He sat very quietly; I could tell that he had a lot on his mind. We talked about his visit with Mr. Smith, and after quite a lot of talking, he said something that stuck in my mind until this very day. Mr. Smith told him that my mother and I could not reside in the same home. We were too volatile to live together because I had started to fight back. I remember thinking that the help that I thought was going to come from talking to Mr. Smith and trusting him with my heart's pain was not coming. All he could say was that my mom and I couldn't live together. Are you kidding me? My father seemed very sad and did not know what to do. I told him not to worry and assured him I wouldn't run away, but I also let him know that I was not going to just sit down and take the abuse—*especially* the physical abuse. He said he understood and would not stop me if I felt that was the only way I could cope. I assured him I would not try to hurt Mom, just to get her off of me and make her stop, somehow. I would focus on other things outside the house since I had about a year and a half until I was 18 and could legally leave home.

I was a very active child and had many interests. I learned to sew in middle school in my home economics class. I made an A-line skirt that was simple, yet classic. I chose a hounds-tooth pattern; blue with a white background. I loved making that skirt and took pride in it when it turned out well. I was a creative child, so when I was expressing that creativity, I felt happy. I went on to sew many of my clothes in high school. My parents could not afford new clothes for us, so many of my clothes came from my sisters. I hated hand-me-downs. My mother even bought clothes for us at our church rummage sale. If any of my friends who had large families wanted to give us clean clothes that were in great shape, she refused! I remember thinking, W*hat is the difference between clothes from my older sisters and clothes from my friend's families?* Both of those would be clean and you would know where they came from, but clothes from a rummage sale were always from an unknown origin.

I took good care of myself growing up. I am sure that I did learn some good things from my mother amidst all the abuse. I know that I learned manners, and I also learned that how you present yourself is important. Being clean, well-groomed, and neat were things that stayed with me. I was excited when I learned to sew because, to me, it was a way out of wearing all the hand-me-downs. I could have a style of my own and not have to wear clothes that belonged to my sisters. Now understand that it first took a few years to make things that could not be worn when they were completed. I followed the directions but did not always understand them. My first project in 7th grade home economics class turned out so well because I had the constant instruction and watchful eye of my teacher. The clothes I made in the next few years after that project were pretty messed up and could not be worn.

I had a lot of help with my sewing through those teen years because of a neighbor. Her name was Mary and she had a machine in her duplex, which was a few houses away. She helped me with my sewing, and she became a safe place to go when the abuse got heavy. She had some small children, which I adored and loved to babysit. Her house wasn't the neatest all the time, but I felt at peace and safe there. She taught me well enough that, when I was in my high school years, I made quite a few stylish and wearable outfits. I was proud to finally be able to make some clothes that I could wear along with finally being able to wear things that were mine and only mine.

Since I made my clothes in high school, I was very observant of how others in my school dressed. It was interesting to see that the kids coming from families with money dressed extremely casual and carefree. The kids from the poor families dressed more expensively. I look back at it now and can see that the kids with money in their families didn't have anything to prove. The kids that came from the poorer families felt that they did. They would wear the more expensive clothes to school to hide the fact they did not have money.

Wearing jeans, flannel shirts, construction shoes, and not wearing a bra was all the rage while I was in high school. While going braless was a normal thing for us teenage girls back then, especially with the wearing of the original halter tops, normally we wore bras in school. We usually went without when hanging out at home and in the neighborhood. So, it was not common for girls to show up to school without a bra—but especially not without makeup.

The kids that came from a family that had little money wore expensive sweatsuits and expensive sneakers, and the girls always had makeup on. When I went to high school, I always had makeup. I did not have much, but I wore it every day. My clothes were mostly sewn by myself, so I was always "styling." As stated earlier, there were six kids in my family and my dad made very little money as a minister. He was pastoring a very small church and we also lived in the parsonage. That took care of a big piece of our living expenses, but it was still very difficult to feed and clothe eight people. I was very happy that I had learned to sew and could make my clothes. When I started working at the age of 16, I kept a small amount of money from my paycheck for sewing supplies and makeup. My dad made me put the rest in the bank. I am glad that he taught me how to manage my money and did not let me spend my whole paycheck instead.

The first job I had was helping my brother with his paper route. We got up early and rode bikes to throw those papers. I got a small stipend for helping him, but the idea is that I learned what it was like to work at a young age. My first official job was in the post office in Bay Shore at the age of 16. I liked the work and the fact that I could make my own money, but there was a lot of overt racism at that job and I remember feeling very uncomfortable. My father would not allow me to quit that job, so I started doing things to get myself fired. I disliked the people and how they acted so much that I felt I had to leave.

My father, being a good minister, believed and instilled in me that there is good and bad in every person. He told me that sometimes, you had to go through a few bad things to get to the good. I will remember that throughout my adult life and teach the same thing to my children. My dad not only spoke these words; his life demonstrated them. It upset him when he witnessed racism and he was always trying to do something about it.

One of the things he did to show me he truly believed in what he taught us was to hold interdenominational services in town. As far as I remember, he was the only minister in the town who was very active in doing so. He especially did this during Thanksgiving time, hosting unity services for all the churches that would participate. He continued to do this until Martin Luther King Jr. was assassinated. I felt that after the assassination happened, the other churches did not want to mix services any longer. People in general were angry at what happened and did not trust each other. You couldn't blame them.

I have fond memories of attending the churches of my friends. Most of my friends while I was growing up were Black. So, as we moved the services around to different denominational churches along with different races, I was able to attend many of my friend's churches. This is when I was first introduced to Black gospel music. We sang hymns in my dad's church. They were beautiful and told great stories, but to me, they were boring. I loved gospel music from the minute I was introduced to it.

I remember when I saw my friends in their choirs singing gospel music, it seemed so different from what I was used to. It seemed to pour from their souls and I was enthralled by it. It also seemed to touch the members of the congregation more deeply than our hymns did. I was surprised to see people clapping along with the music, singing energetically, and getting involved in that music. Needless to say, when the Unitarian services stopped, I was very sad. Things went backward after that. At that time, we had two Black families attending our church, and the Black churches pressured them into leaving our church and attending a Black church in town. I was saddened by that since I believed even as a child that God made all of us different races for a reason and that because He made us that way, we should all worship and live together. Just because our skin was different, I didn't believe that we were all that different from each other.

As far back as I can remember, I always enjoyed friendships with various races of children. There were not many girls in my neighborhood other than my sisters. Due to the abuse that was present in my home, my sisters and I were also abusive to each other. I got into many physical fights with my sister, Bonnie. She was and still is taller than me, large-boned, and thin. She had the strength of a horse. She more often than not won those physical contests between us. So most of my friends were boys both as my playmates and also later in my high school years. I only had two close friends, as I recall, who were girls. I got along well with boys, and since I was a tomboy growing up, I fit right in. Boys at those ages accepted me for who I was. I have always been a touchy-feely kind of person, and when I hung out with the boys, we could tap each other on the arm or push each other a bit and that was fun for us. It seemed very natural for me to be involved in sports growing up. Many of the things my guy friends did were athletic. We climbed trees, played baseball, played tackle football, and played handball together.

There was an element of having a talent for the different sports I participated in. In addition, I was a physical and active child, so it gave me an outlet. I also felt that anything productive that could keep me out of my home and from being beaten was a good thing. I played softball and volleyball in high school. I also attempted soccer in middle school, but remember the girls as being way too rough (my hands got stepped on quite a bit with cleats). I gave up that sport and stuck with volleyball and softball. In high school, all my sports were intramural except track. I seemed to be talented in track and I thoroughly enjoyed it. Since I was petite and had inherited the German build of my mother—large thighs and upper arms—I seemed built to be a sprinter. I excelled at short distances and hurdles. I did not do so well on long distances since they required endurance and a good set of lungs.

I started having asthma at around the age of nine years old. I would wake up and be in the midst of an attack. Back then, they did not have all the wonderful medicines they have today. If it got too hard to breathe, my dad would take me to the emergency room. Many times, I would just have to wait it out and pray that I could breathe easier when I woke up the next morning. The only time I ever missed school was due to an asthma attack. During my teen years, they had just come out with a mist inhaler called Primatene Mist. I remember using that and immediately vomiting. I did not use that for any real-time. I remember thinking many times that I was going to die since I had these long bouts of not being able to breathe very well.

It was hard participating in sports with asthma, but I did it. In addition to the sports played in high school, I also swam. I started swimming lessons at the age of seven. We lived near the water, and there was an abundance of Red Cross swimming lessons that we were enrolled in for free. All six of us children were taught to swim and participated in all levels of the swimming classes every summer. I took every class up to the lifesaver class that would qualify me to be a lifeguard. I stopped there but my sister, Bonnie, went on to take that class and get her certification. I believed that because of my asthma, I would not be a good lifeguard. The swimming did seem to build my lungs up and helped me be a better runner. I was amazed that as a teenager, I could "save" a (cooperating) 250-pound man and do a fireman carry to bring him from the deep end out of the water and do rescue procedures on him—all at a 110-pound weight of my own.

I also participated in karate during my junior and senior years of high school. My boyfriend at the time had several black belts which caused me to be interested in karate. I was also interested in self-defense for me to use later in life as a woman. Karate taught me not only physical control but mental perseverance. In training, you endured physical stress to your body along with being mentally disciplined. Up to this point, I had endured much physical and mental abuse and it felt good to learn something that could help me be mentally strong. Many times people did not understand studying the art of karate and felt that you were trying to learn how to hurt someone or kill someone. Instead, I was learning discipline and a way to protect myself along with getting more physically fit.

This crazy belief was made very clear to me when an incident happened in my own home. I must preface this story by saying that we six children were not the only ones my mom abused. She also abused my father. She used mental abuse tactics along with withholding marital sex to try to control my father. My father was such a kind-hearted and giving man that he would have never put a hand on her, even in self-defense. This particular time, we were in the upstairs hallway of our home. My mother was pushing and hitting my dad. I remember becoming very upset—having known what it feels like to be abused by her for years. I loved my dad very dearly and he was the only "normal" thing in my home. My goal was to get my mom away from him. I wanted to help him. I stood behind him, held both my hands on his waist to stabilize myself, and started kicking around my dad's body to get my mother away from him. Keep in mind that I was not even close to any kind of expert in karate, but I figured if I kicked enough times, she would back off. Eventually, she did, after one of my many kicks landed on the inner thigh of one of her legs. At this point, I told my dad to leave and I would deal with her. I had already had many years of abuse from her hands, thick leather belts, electrical cords, pipes from the vacuum cleaner, wooden spoons, and high-heeled shoes along with the many times she pulled me backward by my long hair.

In the next few days, a really large bruise on her leg rose up. She went around telling anyone who would listen that I tried to kill her. That was her natural assumption since she did not understand karate along with her exaggerating the event. She even threatened to press charges on me and put me in jail. Now isn't that humorous after all the abuse she had bestowed on all six of us kids? I felt as if I could finally stand up and help someone, even when I could not do it for myself. She was attacking someone who I loved with all my heart and he would not hit her even under these awful circumstances. While withstanding all of the abuse from her all those years and not understanding it, I truly could not believe that she would attack another adult, let alone her husband and my father.

It was soon after that event that I started fighting back when my mother hit me. I had had enough and was tired of dealing with it. The abuse that she had bestowed on us all those years made me feel very unworthy, and unloved and convinced me I was a very rotten child. Why would someone abuse us so much if we didn't deserve it? Regardless of those thoughts, something broke in me around 16 or so, and I started fighting back. When I started doing that, she would grab me by my long hair (I wore it usually down to my waist as a teenager) and drag me around. It was very painful along with being very effective at stopping me from hitting her back. I could not get to her as she dragged me around backward by my hair. For many days after this type of incident, I would brush my hair and large clumps of it would come out. It was a crazy and hugely dysfunctional situation.

There were a few times that when she used one of her many weapons of abuse against me, it resulted in a lot of blood. One time, he was extremely angry for some unknown reason and chased me into my bedroom with a high-heeled shoe in her hand. During that era, a high-heeled shoe would have been like the stiletto of today. She cornered me at the side of my bed where I could not escape. She proceeded to beat me in my head with the heel of the shoe. I tried to protect myself with my arms but was not able to stop her from cutting my head severely. I remember leaning on my bedspread while slumped on the floor after she left, crying a lot. I eventually lifted my head and saw a huge bloodstain on the spread. I proceeded to go to the phone and call my father, who was working over in his church office next door. He ran over to the house and got extremely upset at her for doing so much damage to me. He yelled at her that she needed to stop hurting the kids. He helped me wash the wound and took care of my head. He held me and told me he was sorry that he could not stop her from hurting us children. This was one of the many times that I witnessed my dad not knowing what to do to stop her from abusing us children.

As I have been asking God to bring to remembrance the things of my childhood—both good and bad—many things have come back to me. The brain is a wonderful tool, and when you have been alive as long as I have, there is much in it. I believe also that at times we block out some things because there is just so much we deal with. One thing that He brought back to me that I had forgotten about was my high school "sweetheart." Rick was one year older than me. He was very involved in karate, as I stated before. We dated for most of my sophomore, junior, and senior years in high school. He was my first boyfriend that I was intimate with and we were dating for about a year and a half before something transpired between us. We were very close and spent a lot of time together.

As mentioned before, most of my friends were non-Caucasian. Rick was Black. Rick was tall, well-built with all the karate he did, and good-looking. He walked with a proud stride and was very physically strong. Because many of my friends were Black, I thought nothing of dating someone outside my race. I had long ago realized that I was, for some reason, more comfortable dating outside my race. I don't know if it was a difference in the music that I preferred, attitude, culture, or outlook. For some reason, I related to my peers who were non-white more easily than I did with peers of my race.

Rick was one of the boys that most of the girls in high school desired. He was the most sought-after young man in our high school. I believe besides the obvious reason, that it was because his family seemed to be a bit better off than most in our town and he had a car. Having a car while in high school back then was not a given like it somewhat is today. He lived down the street from the high school, so a car was not a necessity for him to get back and forth to school. Many times during school we went to his house for lunch and other things during our senior year. We also did a bit of skipping school to be together. If I haven't mentioned it before, my mother was very strict about our comings and goings. It was hard to get time to spend with Rick. We made a way, and even though it meant skipping some classes, we felt it was necessary.

I want to mention that Rick, while we were together for almost three years, also abused me. He was very strong and I was about 110 pounds when I was in high school. I don't remember when it started or why, but I do remember being pushed and hit on occasion by him. I remembered feeling that it was not right, but in light of what was happening in my home, it seemed normal. I guess at this point I must have felt that I deserved it and was doing things to deserve it. It was not frequent with him, and most of the time he was loving and supportive of all that I was going through on the home front. I just wanted to mention him to state that my mom was not the only one who had hit me in my teenage years.

I want to also mention a few incidents that happened to me when I was a young teen. I was once chased home by Black kids throwing stones at me and my friend. Another time, we were chased home by similar kids with chains. For some reason, she got more of it than I did. I didn't know if it was because I ran faster or if it was more directed at her. I just remember that it was traumatic. The incident that stuck with me more than the others happened at my home. As I said, many different races lived around me. One day, I was in my room on the second floor of my house located at the front of the house. A Black woman was walking down the street on the way down to Main Street. I was looking out the window and decided to call her the n-word. I have no clue why I decided to do that, given that I didn't have a dislike for people outside my race. I guess as a young kid, I did lots of stupid things. I called her that name and then pulled back from the window.

The reason that I am bringing this up is that despite my ignorant behavior, I will never forget her response. She looked up at me and, in a very kind voice, told me that I was not being very nice. She stated that it was not a nice word to use. I felt very bad and said to her that I was sorry. Looking back, I cannot believe that I would do something that stupid, even if my mother was extremely prejudiced. I just remember that when I did that stupid thing, she was so gracious and forgiving in her response to me. This is much like how God treats us—no matter how stupid and unkind the things that we do to others, He is merciful and forgiving to us. She taught me that no matter how the other kids who were misguided (as I was in that moment) treated me, there is a better way to respond.

This would be put to the test in my years in high school. Because I was dating Rick, I got confronted many, many times by some of the Black girls in school. They were jealous that he was dating me, a white girl, instead of one of them. Numerous times I was confronted by groups of Black girls. They were outside the group of Black kids that I hung with. I mentioned that I had mostly guy friends, and maybe this was one of the reasons why. I didn't relate to girls and all of their drama very well. When a group would come up to me, they would accuse me of calling someone in their family a bad name. Usually, I did not know them or their family members. They would push me and dare me to hit them back. Now, I may not have been very old, but I also was not stupid. I knew that if I fought back, it would be all of them against one of me and I would lose that battle. I had no desire to end up in the hospital, so I allowed them to push me around. Besides, they couldn't do anything to me that hadn't already been done to me by my mother. I would have better odds fighting back with her.

This kind of incident happened to me several times. I did not fight back and usually ran from fighting. Most of these incidents happened in the school. Many times, I believed that it was best to keep these incidents to myself. I do remember that I did go to the school administration a few times, but once again did not feel as if authority figures helped or protected me. A few times, these incidents happened on my way home from school. Several happened as I was carrying my violin home with me. I had my instrument with me a lot since I played in the orchestra at the high school along with doing musical accompaniments for the high school plays that we performed. My dad paid for me to have private lessons as I grew up because I did exhibit quite a bit of talent in that area. So, as I had my violin a lot with me on the way home, it got damaged a few times when I was attacked. When I wouldn't fight these girls back, they would push me down and also damage my instrument. I remember worrying that I was going to get in trouble at home for the violin getting damaged. I was more upset about that than the fact that these kids were threatening my safety.

One of the activities that I did to stay away from home was to act in our yearly high school play and play my violin. I am surprised now that I was good enough to be in the Long Island Symphony as a teenager. There were about six or seven of us that played with all the older people. In addition to this, I was able to play difficult music that was scored for the plays we did. I acted in "My Fair Lady" and also played in the small orchestra accompanying the "Mame" play we did. We also had state competitions that my private violin instructor had me compete in yearly. We would play before a judge and they would grade us in many different areas of music based on our performance. I remember feeling very scared to go before these judges but looking back, maybe this helped me. I was excelling in another area of my life besides sports. I was talented and it gave me something that helped me feel good about myself. I also sang, since I was a small girl and did many solos growing up. I also remember in high school, my private violin teacher (Mr. Atherton) had me practicing Tchaikovsky—listening to an LP "Long Playing Record," while I read and played the music from the written music.

My mother also grew up with a love of music and was an excellent soprano singer. She received a voice scholarship that made it so she was able to go to college. Music was very important to her. I remember that she was a paid soloist in many different churches in the towns around my hometown while I was growing up. Before the cuts in the budget of today's schools, we had many music classes in school. We learned to read music and play instruments. All children were introduced to music and had the opportunity to play an instrument if they wanted to. Along with my mom being so talented, my father was, too. He was able to play the piano and organ and did so from a young age. I remember there were many times that I played my violin and he played the piano in our home. He was so talented and would usually accompany me without using the music I was playing—he would do it by hearing my music. I would later in life learn that he played by ear and not by actually reading the music.

I truly believe that having these varying interests despite my abuse at home is what allowed me to grow up with a sense of balance and worth. I was being told and shown at home that I was not worth anything. Outside the home, I was being shown that I was gifted in many areas and could find pleasure in these things. Of course, since a home is where you get your main programming in your character and self-worth, I listened more to what was coming from the home front. I tried to escape it as much as possible, but those feelings were embedded in my emotions and heart. I believe that this is the reason that when certain things happened to me that were unjust, at times, I did not stand up for myself or even question whether they should be happening.

If anyone were to ask me if I was ever molested, I would always answer with a resounding, "No, thank God!" To me, parents or adult family members that sexually molest kids are just unforgivable. I always remember feeling throughout my life, when I heard stories of this happening, that I was lucky to have not experienced that. I would have rather been beaten, even though I am sure the feelings that I felt and the ones children who have been sexually traumatized felt are similar. We feel confused, not understanding why adults who have been put in charge of us would abuse us in such a manner. How could people who were in our lives to protect us and teach us how to properly act do something so horrible to us? Not only were they not teaching us the right things and making us feel helpless, they taught us that we did not matter. We did not have a voice or deserve one.

Now, in writing this book, God is bringing to remembrance that one time I was sexually molested. I realize it was nothing like what most kids go through, but it needs to be spoken about. I was a teenager when this occurred. As mentioned earlier, I studied karate during my junior and senior years in high school. I mostly took classes at a "dojo" located in a nearby town. My dad made sure I got back and forth to these classes. I believe that he wanted me to be involved in as many activities outside the home for much of the same reasons as I felt. I also took a class at the YMCA. I remember one time, I was alone in the office of the YMCA instructor. It was after class and he was answering a question I had about self-defense. He used this opportunity to show me what I could do if someone came up and grabbed my breasts. Of course, he had to grab my breasts to show me how to defend against that kind of assault, didn't he?

I remember feeling violated but unsure. I never mentioned this to anyone because I was unsure whether it was inappropriate or whether anyone would believe me. After all, the police believed that my mother could treat me any kind of way as long as I had a roof over my head and bread and water in my belly. Why would anyone believe me if I confided in someone that I felt funny about what he did? It was not until many years later that I realized that I was violated. Now, please understand I am in no way comparing this to the sexual abuse of many people that was repeated and carried on against them for many years. I cannot fathom how I would have felt to have suffered that. I can only imagine what that felt like. I only bring this up to let you know when you are being abused in any manner, we seem to not know where the boundaries are. We are unclear about where those lines are and sometimes allow things to happen to us without standing up for ourselves. I never stood up for myself against that incident or the times that my boyfriend felt he needed to be physical with me—none of those times were appropriate. We get confused as to where our boundaries are and they become blurry. This is not our fault and we have to forgive ourselves for some things that happen to us. We also have to forgive ourselves for not standing up against them. We also have to forgive those who have harmed us, mainly to help ourselves heal.

I remember that even though I could not stand up for myself, I was quick to stand up for others. A particular incident comes to mind with my best friend who came to visit me at my home. I did not allow many kids to visit me in my home because I was afraid they would suffer some verbal abuse by my mother. While I did share with my friends what was going on in my home, I did not want them to see me being abused or risk her saying something to them. Valerie was my best friend growing up, and we had been friends since we were seven years old. Her family came to our church and, like ours, they had at least six kids. One Sunday, after church, she came over to see me. I believe that my mom did not know she was there. She came yelling and screaming into my bedroom. Val heard her coming and hid behind my bedroom door. I do not know what my mother was upset about, and at that point in my life, it did not matter. It seemed it was always something and what mattered at that point to me was that my friend was there.

Valerie, being my best friend, had heard plenty from me about my mother. I think she thought I was exaggerating or being overly dramatic. When my mother came yelling at me into my room, I could see Val behind the door with a look of fear on her face. I remember thinking that no matter what Mom was upset about, I needed to appease her and get her out of my room as soon as possible. I know that we were in our early teens, as we were beginning to develop and it was the summertime. Again, I do not remember why my mother was upset, but it was of the utmost importance to me to stem the tirade and get her out of my room. It was my mom's habit to barge into my room at any time and I did not have any privacy in my room. I am not sure if my mom hit me during that incident, but I do remember Val's reaction to it. She not only believed it was as bad as I had been telling her but also felt what it was like to go through it. All I remember was feeling horrified that my friend witnessed that and felt even smaller because of it.

Another incident happened during my junior year at my home with my friend Cheryl. We called her "Candy" and we ran track together. Her mom was like a second mother to me, though she was much different than mine. I remember that she was a loving, caring, and very committed Christian woman. She was what a mother was supposed to be. She was an important thread in the fabric of the positive side of my childhood and remains a dear person to me to this day. I stated earlier that I did not usually bring any of my friends to my home. That was solidified by the incident mentioned above with Val.

One day, I decided to allow another close friend, Candy, to come into my home. I had to run home to pick up something, so I figured that we would only be there a few minutes. Again, my friends believed me that what I shared with them was going on at home, but thought I was possibly exaggerating. We walked into my kitchen and my mother was doing dishes at the sink—one of the few times I remember her doing any housework in my teen years. My mother said hello but treated her as if she had some disease. She also said something inappropriate, and I don't remember quite what it was. I only remember that it was very uncomfortable for me and Candy. I remember feeling protective of her and embarrassed for her. I apologized to her and got what I came home for, then hurried out of the home. Candy said to me that she did not realize my mother was as bad as I had been telling her.

My mother was not only abusive to her kids, but she also was mean to the kids that she taught as well. For many years, my mother was a substitute teacher. While she attended school to get her certificate to become certified as a teacher, she did work substituting many different subjects. While music was her forte, she was asked to teach in many different schools and classes. Candy reminded me recently that a friend of hers got so mad at her for being mean to them that he locked her in a closet. I had forgotten about that, but after her telling me about it again, I remember feeling happy at that time because someone had stood up against my mother. I am sure that boy got into a lot of trouble, but I am sure he felt good about what he had done. It was hard enough to endure what was going on in my home, but also hearing from all the kids who knew me that my mother was mean and overly controlling in the classes she taught was embarrassing.

As you can imagine, me being both abused and a preacher's kid, I was no angel. Many of my behaviors were a way to push back and rebel against what was happening to me. It angered me that I was being treated this way by my mother while also being on "stage" with the members of our church. Since we lived in the parsonage, my father had a phone that was his office phone and had an extension in our home. That phone rang many times from the parishioners calling my dad to report things about us kids. One time, an elderly member called my dad to report that they had seen me cross the street in between the lights on Main Street. I couldn't believe that people were so petty. They called about many other things also.

One time I came through the hallway where the phone was located on the way to our living room. My dad was on the phone and I could see him shaking. He got off the phone and came to get me. He said that someone called—he wouldn't tell me who—accusing me of having sexual relations with my boyfriend. I do not know how this person would even know this enough to be telling my father this news. Most of the times that Rick and I were together were at lunch at his parent's home. Of course, I denied this to my father because I did not want him to know that. I did not care what my mother felt about me but was always very concerned about what my dad felt. He was the positive parent in my life and I never wanted to disappoint him. I needed his love very much since I didn't feel any from my mom. I did not want to lie to him but felt it was necessary not to hurt him or look less in his eyes. I felt furious that someone would call my father and bother him with something like this. Things like this happened often because we were preacher's children. We could go nowhere in town without someone seeing us.

I remember being down on Main Street in my young teens behind a store, trying to smoke a cigarette. Someone from the church saw me and proceeded to tell my dad. He asked me about it later and I was truthful with him. It made me sick and I truly don't know what I was thinking, being an asthmatic and trying to smoke. He was upset but not angry at me. He understood and was glad that I tried it and had gotten sick from it. Besides, how angry could he get when he smoked three to four packs a day? When I had my asthma attacks, I could not go anywhere near my dad. He was always smoking and had many cigarettes that burned up in his ashtray. When I would go visit him in his office next door at the church, I would always see his large ashtray with many cigarette butts in it. There would always be one burning in the holder. I truly believe that he could not physically smoke too many cigarettes in a day, but he was a chain smoker.

I received my license when I was about 17 years old. My dad had taught me to drive in his Cadillac. Since these were the type of cars my dad owned, I had no other choice but to learn to drive in a big car. I took a driver's education class at school, but my dad let me practice in his car. I even had to take my driver's test in his car. Keeping in mind that I was about 5'2" and weighed about 110 pounds, I was a petite girl in a big Cadillac. When the instructor got in the car, he made a joke about how he usually had big kids taking the test in a small car. Since my legs were so short, I had my dad's front seat up as far as it could go. When he got in the front seat to administer a driving test, his knees were all the way squished up against the glove box.

Another bad thing I did was steal my mother's car. She and my dad were out, it was daytime, and I don't remember if I had some specific place to go. I somehow got the keys to my mother's car and decided to go on an errand. As I learned much later in life, all things done in the "dark" will come out in the "light." I was driving down a busy street, and it was pouring rain. A dog ran out into the street in front of the car that was driving in front of me. The car in front of me hit their brakes. I, being an inexperienced driver, hit my brakes, but did not pump them. I slid into the back right corner of that car in front of me. I started freaking out since I had my mom's car without permission. The police that showed up on the scene called my dad. Then I knew I was really in trouble. Since my dad was a minister in the community, he knew a lot of similar public servants—police and firemen alike. Of course, the police officer who showed up at the scene knew my dad.

As you probably can imagine, I got in a lot of trouble. I was grounded and had to pay for the repair of my mother's old car. I should have realized from all the other things that happened to me that a preacher's daughter was not going to do much without being seen by someone who knew her dad. I guess I had to give it the "old college" try. In justifying my actions, this was the worst thing that I did. I know that I was acting out and pushing my boundaries (since they seemed to be so constrictive). In no way am I saying that what I did was right—we all know stealing is wrong. I think through the years though, and especially after raising my four kids, I could relate a bit with them when they felt as if they had to act out. I did not abuse them as I had been abused, but I realized through them that all kids try their boundaries. Later in life, in therapy, I would have to analyze what was done to me and what I did as a teenager. This would help me to heal from all of this hurt and become emotionally healthier.

Chapter Three
My Father

My father was born on May 24th, 1913 in Flint, Michigan. I do not remember ever meeting his parents, and now realize they died soon after I was born. My father was an older dad, marrying my mother when he was 32 years old and she was 19. He had his first child with my mother at the age of 37, five years after they had married. He had six children with my mother, the last being born in 1969. The remaining five children were born about one and a half years apart. So, there were six kids born to my mother and father in approximately nine years.

As it has been mentioned earlier in this book, my father had been married before marrying my mother. He was married for about five years with his first wife and had two sons. I did not find out this information until I was a senior in high school. I was surprised, to say the least, but I figured that my mom did not want him to tell us. In addition, we had not had many visits with my father's sisters, so I was led to believe this was all due to my mom. A few years ago, my younger sister met with the second son of my father's first marriage and found out some information about him, his wife, and his family.

My father and my mother met in Philadelphia. My mother was 19 and in college—specifically Beaver College on a voice scholarship (now called Arcadia). Their courtship lasted about a year and they were married when she was 19. They were very much in love, and from what we have been told and observed, the first five years of their marriage were the happiest years for them.

I have always felt that my dad loved being a father. It was difficult having so many children—a total of eight—but he seemed happy when he was around us. I know he felt a lot of stress being married to my mother after the kids started coming. Due to the abusive nature of my mother's disciplining for us kids, along with the abuse that she bestowed on my father, it was difficult for my dad to be happy a lot. The only time I saw him happy was when he was with his parishioners or taking us somewhere.

I cannot imagine what it was like for him to take all six of us in the car somewhere since we bickered a lot. He said many times that he was not going to do it ever again, but he always did. We enjoyed being around our father because of his personality. He tried to be upbeat most of the time. He had a great sense of humor and was always laughing a lot, whenever possible.

When I remember my dad, I recall a caring, giving, merciful, and forgiving man. He had a wonderful sense of humor, along with a youthful spirit. He was always cracking jokes and making people laugh. He was great at being real, open, honest, and transparent with everyone. He was not a judgmental person and was very kind. He did not think he was better than anyone. He felt that no matter what you had done in your life, God still loved you and everyone deserves second chances in life.

I do not know how my siblings feel, but for me, my dad saved my life. I cannot imagine what would have become of me had he not been around. He was protective of us as much as he could be. No matter what Mom did to us, he tried to stop her without ever touching her. He was a gentleman and believed that even if Mom was hitting him, he could not hit her back. He intervened whenever possible, but it was very difficult for him to be home all the time. He took his calling and job as a minister very seriously. When something bad happened to us, he would come home immediately. When he wasn't visiting and taking care of his parishioners, he was working long hours in the church office. Since we lived next to the church, I remember knocking on the office door many times to obtain my father's help. It did not matter what time of day or night it was. He was always there for all six of us children, and I believe did the best he knew how.

My dad was a true buffer between us children and our mom. Many times he interrupted her abuse by trying to give us a resemblance of a normal life. I always felt that no matter what, my dad loved me and supported me. I knew in my heart that whatever I needed, my dad would try hard to get it for me.

All this craziness took place back in the sixties and seventies. Back then, people did not easily divorce. In addition, as a minister, I feel that he was unable to break up our family. Before his death at 87, he told his closest friend that his biggest regret in his life was not getting away from the abuse. At that time, we all said that we did not hold that against him, feeling that during that time it would not have been possible.

I have very beautiful memories of Dad and me playing music together. All of us sang from a very early age and played some sort of instrument. I started playing the violin at the age of nine and played until I graduated high school. Money was limited for him and our family, but he made a sacrifice to get me private lessons.

I guess he saw a gift there and wanted to nourish it. I remember being taken once a week to a nearby town for an hour. My teacher's name was Mr. Atherton. I know that both my dad and Mr. Atherton were often frustrated with me. Even though I was very talented, I hated practicing. I often heard about how gifted I was and how private lessons were expensive. I tried to practice often, but I am sure I did not practice enough. I learned quickly, and by the time I was a junior and senior in high school, I was playing in the Long Island Symphony orchestra. This orchestra consisted of older, more professional members along with only five or six high schoolers.

Some of the best times with my dad involved us sharing our love for music. Dad had natural abilities and would play along with me. I would use music, playing, and reading along while he played by ear. It was a beautiful thing to see and to hear. My last time seeing my dad about six months before he died was at his home in Mojave, California. The last thing I saw him doing that time was playing his keyboard. He was 87 when he died and had bad vision. He was playing his Casio, adding background instruments, and playing for hours. Music was an integral part of him and never ceased to feed his soul. I learned my love of music from him.

My dad meant a lot to many other people outside of his family. Many parishioners thought the world of my dad. Many times throughout the 50 years that he was in the ministry, he was there for them and their families. To this day, I hear the stories about how when they lost a family member or had some tragedy take place, my dad would be at their side. He would sometimes spend days with them, helping them to grasp what was happening and comforting them.

Dad also was a social person and spoke to strangers easily. At his memorial service, I heard many stories of other lives that he saved. Alcoholics Anonymous met in our church weekly, and Dad would do whatever it took to make sure that he was around in his office every week at the end of the meeting. He would come out and speak to the people attending the meetings. He would not judge them, and would instead show them love. He asked them all the time if they wanted to talk, and if they did that he would be there for however long they needed him. He led many to the Lord and to survive their challenges with mercy, grace, and understanding.

One of the things I truly loved about my dad was that you knew he was not perfect, and he never tried to be something he wasn't. He was real, honest, and very forthright about his shortcomings. He taught me a love that I now know as Agape—unconditional love. It is the same type of love that God feels for us. No matter when we do wrong, or how many times we fall short of expectations, God loves me and everyone else just the same.

On the outside, those who knew him could see his faults, just like any of us. The difference about him is that on the inside, he was pure. He showed me the mercy, grace, and forgiveness that I know came from his relationship with the Lord. My dad demonstrated how the Lord loves us and treats us regardless of what we do.

My father fostered the tools and characteristics of my personality that I, along with my five siblings, needed to survive years of abuse from my mother. I know now that these tools were given to me by God because, in His infinite wisdom, He knew that I would need them. It is said that "hurt people, hurt people." I have learned that through the years and realized just how much my dad saved me from going over the "deep end."

I will be forever grateful that the Lord gave me such a man to raise me and to be my dad. I loved him dearly and appreciated him more. I know that I did not show him that while I was growing up, but I hope that at some level he knew that while he was alive. I was in awe of what he could do, his priorities, and how he survived the constant challenges that were put into his path.

I am sure that there were many times that our family was criticized. My mom, for many years, was a paid soloist in different churches. She was not your "typical" minister's wife. For many years that I can remember, she did not come to church with us or support my dad. It surprised me, and the family took a lot of flak for it. To this day, I still have people who will cross my path when I go back to Long Island and will talk badly about my dad. Of course, it is only a small handful, but isn't it amazing how a few people can poison a large group with their bitterness and negativity?

In 2010, I left Colorado and moved back to living on Long Island. I will discuss my mother's Alzheimer's and my reasons for coming back in another chapter. I was participating in a holiday craft fair back at the old church where my dad ministered for 20 years. It was a bit weird to go back there and do that since I had not lived back on the island since I was a teenager.

I do a lot of sewing, and sometimes I make what are called "heat bags." I love to sew and these heat bags are easy to make, yet necessary in many people's lives. You put them in the microwave for three minutes or so and the popcorn (or rice, for moist heat) heats up and stays warm for 20-30 minutes. I have been making these bags for years and sold them solely to close friends and coworkers. I decided to try and sell them at craft fairs this first fall when I was back on Long Island. I signed up to participate in the Christmas fair at the church, selling my heat bags.

I knew that going back and participating in something that I attended as a child could be a bit emotional. I prayed about it, and knew that God would give me the strength of mind and character to do it. Deep inside, I knew that this was just something I needed to do to go "full circle" down the path of my journey. The sale was for Friday evening and all day Saturday. During the afternoon on Saturday, when customer flow was a bit slow, I went to the other vendor tables to see what was for sale. I wanted to possibly purchase some items for Christmas gifts for my kids and grandchildren.

As I was walking around, I came to a table that had handmade items on it. Most of the items were knitted and I was told that a church member who was currently 101 years old made them. I found a vest that looked as if it would fit one of my granddaughters. It was beautiful and reasonably priced. I told her I grew up in the church years ago and my father was a past minister. She instantly made a nasty face upon learning who I was. Her first words to me were: "I was not a fan of his." She proceeded to tell me that she left the church and did not come back until he left to preach in California. I asked her why and she told me it was over something he said from the pulpit.

She continued to tell me a relative of hers was on the board that hired my dad when he came to preach there. She also told me stories about things that she had heard about him. Of course, this was mega-gossip, and while I don't participate in gossip—nor should any Christian—I continued to talk to her. I resented that she was wrong in most of her information and my dad was not around to defend himself. After all, he died ten years before this incident. The typical thing about gossip is that most of the time it is not the correct information. I started to talk about each thing she brought up and let her know that her information was incorrect. Most of what she assumed with her misinformation was incorrect accusations against my dad. These accusations were accurate about my mom, though, and I let her know that.

She shocked me with most of the accusations, but one of them caught me off-guard. Even if she believes this to be true about my dad, it should never have been spoken to his daughter. She asked me how I felt about my father being gay. It took me a minute, and I said to her that he was not. I can understand that some of the people that my dad helped by bringing them to the U.S. and helping them get citizenship put him in a position of others thinking he might be gay.

I did get a chance to talk to my dad about these things later in his life. We were fairly open about all things, so one day when I was visiting him out in California, we had that discussion. I told him that if that is what he had decided to do I would not judge him for it, since I am far from perfect (like most of us). He looked right into my eyes and said, "No, I have never done that." He explained that he was curious about it because being with my mother made him bitter and heartbroken. But even though the temptations were in front of him at different times in his life, he had never done that.

At the time that we were discussing this, he had been in a long-term relationship/close friendship with a woman. I know as you are reading this you are probably laughing at me. Does it sound as if I am making excuses? Well, I understand if you feel that way, but I am not. I am only giving you facts as I know them. I am not trying to rewrite anyone's history here, just giving the facts as they happened. The purpose of this is to share with you the people in my life who shaped me and the challenges I had to survive.

Again, as stated earlier, my dad was far from perfect. He was real about who he was and who he wasn't. He did not pretend to be something else and was very honest about that. He loved and helped many people through many of the challenges they faced. I was shocked that this person was still talking trash about my dad some 30 years later. I do not want to judge anyone and try very hard not to. I "judge not lest ye be judged." I just want to share with you a fact—it is sad to me that people can go to church for years and years and still not learn about forgiveness, not judging others, and trying to love others as God loves us. I feel like we go to church to learn God's Word, congregate amongst other Christians, and get better as time goes on. So even though we continue to be imperfect, I have a hard time understanding that these actions could continue after years of going to church.

I do feel sorry for people who continue to gossip, have bitterness in their hearts, and do not learn about true forgiveness. I think that my dad showed me an important lesson—not to judge others and try to remain positive. Life is a choice! I can't control what others do to me, but I can control how I react. Thank you, Dad, for teaching me that no matter how people treat me or what they say about me, I can choose to believe that I am who God says I am. I can choose to be positive as much as possible every day!

To this day, I miss my dad very much. No matter how many times I messed up, he loved me through it all. He was always there for all of my siblings as well. We all know that he did the best he knew how, and he was there for us day in and day out when we needed him. I love my father very much and certainly look forward to the day God calls me home so I can see him again. I know Heaven is an awesome place, and it is a lot more fun and special because he is there having fun and making others smile!

Chapter Four

My Abusive Marriage

I was married at the age of 19 years old; in fact, it was on my 19th birthday. At 18 years old, I went into the army. I went to basic training in Mobile, Alabama. After basic, I had several advanced job training sessions. First, I went to Fort Ord in California for clerk training. I then went to Fort Benjamin Harrison in Indianapolis, Indiana. While at Fort Ord, we were getting up at five A.M. and standing out in damp, cold weather. I have never been a morning person. With the combination of the early hours and the foggy, damp weather, I kept getting sick with bad colds. I had sore throats and coughs that lasted for quite some time.

By the time I arrived at Fort Benjamin Harrison (Ft Ben), my immune system was weak. I thought that I was better but I was not. At Fort Ben, I went out dancing at the NCO Club quite a bit. My girlfriend and I, who was also in training with me to be a personnel management specialist, went out regularly. We would go to the club on base or go away for the weekend with friends, renting a car to get around. After a few weeks there (and lots of lack of sleep), I became sick again. This time, I was having trouble walking on top of being extremely tired. I finally went on a "sick call" and had some blood drawn by a handsome lab technician. His name was Ed and he was very good at drawing blood. I remember telling him not to hurt me or I would use my good arm to hit him! (A very lady-like thing to say.)

He smiled at me and told me that he thought I was very sick and the lab tests would prove that. I told him that I had a game that I had to be in—softball or volleyball; I cannot remember. I had to be well in the next few days. They ran a few tests on me and found out that I had mononucleosis (often known as just mono). I did not know much about the sickness except that I was feeling really tired. I was still out partying at the NCO club, just not as much. A few days later, I saw Ed out with one of his buddies. I was wearing a mini dress that was the style back then. My friend was wearing the same dress as me but hers was brown and mine was blue. The dress was very short with matching panties that went underneath.

When Ed saw me, he was surprised that I was out and not back in the barracks in bed. I called him "Doc" because the uniform he wore was white and reminded me of a doctor. He told me that my test had immediately shown positive and that I was a very sick young lady. Of course, with my "New York attitude," I told him he was crazy and I was not that sick. Not much was going to stop me from being out with my friends. I did not like this guy Ed; I thought that he was someone who thought he knew everything. Whenever I saw him at the club, he was having a drink and sitting with his friends. I also did not care for his friends. One of them had commented to me that I was just another "wannabe sister" (a White girl acting like a Black one). At the time that he said that, Ed was trying to talk to me and had my hand in his. It made me so mad that I pulled my hand from Ed's and walked away.

I did get sicker, so very soon, I was having trouble walking again. With mononucleosis, sometimes you have liver issues. With me, I had problems with my legs. It was winter at that time when we were at Ft Ben. We were wearing uniforms that were shirts and skirts and our legs got very cold. Along with the cold, the muscles in my legs were not working correctly. It made it very difficult for me to walk to personnel management school and to go to the mess hall to eat. Some of my friends helped me and I tried to get a ride whenever possible. I remember being very surprised that I was having issues with my legs since I was in excellent shape and still very athletic.

The last night there before I was going back to Fort Ord—where I was going to be stationed—I ran into Ed at the NCO Club. He asked me to dance and I figured since it was my last night there, what would be the harm? We danced a few dances, with the "bump" being the main one. We both liked to dance and danced well together. He later asked me if I wanted a drink and I remember having one since I still had to finish packing to leave the base in the morning. We sat and talked and I found out that he seemed to be a nice guy after all. He appeared to like me and wanted me to call/write to him after I left.

Ed walked me back to my barracks and we stood on the porch for a long time. It was freezing and he offered me his jacket along with sitting close so that we could stay warm. We talked about many things and seemed to have a lot in common. We talked about our families and what we wanted to get from being in the military. We stayed out there until at least three or four in the morning. I went in then to finish packing, as my flight was leaving pretty early. We said goodbye and promised to keep in touch. At that point, some feelings were starting within me and they were of a nature that I had never felt before.

I left that morning and went back to Fort Ord. Ed and I stayed in touch frequently by phone and letters. Remember, there were no computers or email back in 1973! A short time after I left Ft Ben, I went back there to see Ed. We were looking forward to seeing each other since our feelings had grown through our correspondence. I was so excited to see him and as soon as I got there, he got me settled into the guest house on base. We went out to eat, went dancing, and talked for hours. I stayed there visiting for a few days and by the time I was getting ready to leave, he asked me to marry him. We had only been dating for about three months. I was very much already in love with him, so I said yes. He was not able to get me a ring at that time, so he picked one out shortly after that and mailed it to me. It was a simple and pretty solitaire.

I was excited to be engaged and planning a wedding. We continued to see each other every six to eight weeks, taking turns seeing each other at our respective bases. We decided to get married on my birthday, October 13th, in New York. My dad would officiate at the wedding and we would have a simple reception in the fellowship hall at my home church. Nobody involved had much money, so we were going to try to make it as uncomplicated and lovely as we could. I made my dress in white satin fabric with some embellishments. My best friend, Valerie, was wearing the same style of dress as me but in a blue fabric without all the embellishments.

I was busy and happy with the wedding and all of the preparations. I sent out invitations and we decided that the reception would be easygoing. We ordered a wedding cake, but the food was prepared and brought in by members of the church. We set up the hall ourselves and kept the decorations very plain. I had a real flower bouquet, along with one for Valerie and boutonnieres for the men. We both had one person standing up with us. My dad walked me down the aisle and then officiated while wearing his minister robes. Ed's family drove in from Chicago to attend. There were about 150 people in attendance for both the wedding and the reception.

The beginning of our challenges started with flying home for the wedding. By this time, Ed had moved bases from Fort Ben to the Tripler Medical Center on the island of Oahu, Hawaii. I was still at Fort Ord. We were supposed to meet in San Francisco and fly home together to Bay Shore, New York. He was taking a military hop so scheduling proved to be a bit tricky. I took the bus to San Francisco on the appointed date only to get there and find out he was not able to get on that army flight. He tried another one and got bumped from that one too. I had to take the bus back down to Fort Ord and ride it again the next day back up to San Francisco. Finally, later that night, he made it to San Francisco. We were able to get on a flight the next morning to New York together. We were arriving a week early to get things done for the wedding, so we had a few days to spare.

We arrived in New York safely and went about finishing up wedding preparations. The day of the wedding came, and everyone was getting ready. The men had gotten dressed and were standing by in the choir room of the church. I grew up in the parsonage, so we were right next door in my bedroom getting dolled up. As my maid of honor and I were making final dressing preparations, my oldest sister, Beth, asked me if I wanted her to press my dress. It had traveled from California and had a few wrinkles. I was happy to have the help and she proceeded to iron it. She placed the iron right over where the dress would lay over my abdomen and screamed. As she picked up the iron, a piece of the dress melted on the bottom of the iron.

There was a lot of confusion as to what to do next. I was a seamstress in high school, making most of my clothes. I still had a drawer full of scrap material in my bedroom dresser. I went to the drawer and started rummaging through my scraps. I found some white cotton material and prepared to hand sew a patch behind the hole the iron had burned into the dress. Then I took some mantilla lace (the kind that I had used to make my veil) and put it down the middle front of the dress. I finished it off with some fabric lace trim. You could not tell—unless you looked very closely—that there was ever an accident with my dress.

While all of this was going on, no one bothered to tell the groom what was happening. He was thinking that maybe he had been left at the altar. The organist kept getting up and getting more music from his organ bench. The people were wondering what was taking so long. I finally sent word to the church next door that we had an accident with the dress that was being fixed and we would be over soon. I believe it was about three hours that the wedding was delayed. It is a good thing that the church was the one I grew up in, with the minister being my dad and the reception being in the fellowship hall. Otherwise, the time delay could have been a major financial issue.

Finally, with the dress repairs completed, we got married. I was very happy that day and all the days following. We went off and spent our wedding night at a local hotel. We were leaving shortly to go back to our separate bases, but we had already put in papers for a compassionate reassignment. Since we were now a married couple, the army was going to move me over to Hawaii where Ed was stationed. We flew back to San Francisco together wearing matching outfits. We had tan suede dressy overalls with matching polyester print shirts. We were just too cute and very much in love. Remember that this was October 1973 before you "laugh" at our outfits! The main point was that we were so much in love that we were wearing matching clothes.

A few months after we had been married, my reassignment finally came through. I was going to be moving to Hawaii to be with my husband. I was very excited! Ed had still been living in the barracks, but as soon as I got there, we would be looking for an apartment. We both were going to get marriage stipends and allowances to be able to afford the housing in Hawaii. As soon as I got there, some friends of his offered to put us up in their house for two months until our allowances came in. We accepted. We were both happy to be together again and were looking forward to finally starting our lives together. The house we were staying in was about 15-20 minutes from our bases. He was stationed at Tripler Army Medical Center and I was up the road at Fort Shafter. He was still a medical laboratory technician and I was a personnel management specialist. I would be working with a military intelligence unit.

It was while we were staying with these friends that things started to go wrong. I am not sure how or why, but about a month after I arrived in Hawaii, Ed and I got into an argument that ended with him hitting me. I was in shock. Looking back, I probably should have walked out or separated from him right then. I think because he had never shown signs of being abusive during our courtship, I did not understand what had happened to change things. In addition, since I was so abused as a child by my mother, I thought that I did something wrong. Even though I was an adult, I was still thinking at that time that I got hit because I did something to deserve it. I had a very low self-esteem due to the abuse bestowed on me over all those years by my mother.

We moved into our apartment, and the abuse happened again. The attacks occurred about every two to three months, so I was still trying to figure out what was wrong. Ed was a moody person, and I learned to leave him alone to let him unwind alone when he came home from work. I would wait a few hours before speaking to him. I also learned, in visiting his work, that he had two personalities. He was kind and competent while he was at the workplace. Meanwhile, at home, he was sometimes nice and other times very volatile. I am sure that if his coworkers were told of what was happening behind closed doors in our apartment, they would have had a hard time believing it.

We continued going out together, dancing and partying at our friends' houses. We were very much in love and went everywhere together. Whenever Ed had an outburst, we would try to make up and go on. However, his outbursts did not only include hitting me. It also included taking some of my clothes or other items that I had made with my own hands and destroying them. I did not understand the physical or mental abuse that he was deploying on me.

One time, we paid for his mom to come visit from Chicago. I loved his family, and his mom was like a second mother to me. We got along well and had great times together. It was hard to convince her to leave Chicago to go on vacation to Hawaii to see us, and I was so happy that she was there. Ed got mad at me one evening and started acting up. I was banging on the door of one of our bedrooms, asking him to please come out and talk to me. He got so upset that he threw open the door and punched me in the side of my right eye. His mother was sitting right there watching everything, and I am sure was shocked when he punched me. I was embarrassed for him, but I was also thinking that if she had believed I was exaggerating his abuse over the phone before this event, she now knew that I had been telling her the truth.

Since he punched me pretty hard on the side of my right eye, by morning the right eye was severely black and blue. I had a nasty shiner and had to wear sunglasses over my eyes to go to work. I used the standard excuse of running into a door as the reason I was wearing sunglasses to cover up my black eye. I did confide in one person who worked with my husband, but they had a really hard time believing that he hit me. He had such a different façade at work that it was virtually unbelievable that he would be the type that would beat me at home. It took a while for that black and blue eye to heal, and it was a huge embarrassment to me. Even though I had been hit many times before, it was especially shameful that this time there was proof of the abuse left for everyone to see. Most of the hits that Ed showered me with were in the head or the body where you would not see the bruises.

Along with the physical abuse, Ed was starting to mentally abuse me. If we got into an argument while driving home from some event, he would kick me out of the car and tell me to walk home. I did so on many occasions, and I would not say much when I finally arrived home. That was especially frustrating since we only had one car. It was belittling when I was kicked out and had to walk the rest of the way home. I hoped that no one that I knew ever saw me. Many times, it was quite a long walk, and so it was very tiring for me. I didn't dare say anything when I finally got home for fear of being physically abused.

The abuse continued as we moved from Hawaii to San Antonio, Texas. We were married for about two years when this happened. We had been to a bit of counseling where I had let Ed know that if things didn't change, I was going to file for a divorce. I did not believe in divorce, but I was fearful for my life and felt that one day he was going to put me in the hospital. I asked him many times to go to counseling if he was interested in keeping the marriage together. I don't remember what the arguments or outbursts were about and didn't understand why he felt the need to hit me at all.

When we moved to San Antonio, things got worse. The attacks increased in frequency. We had some friends that we were stationed with in Hawaii that later moved to San Antonio. One time, Ed got mad at me and ran up the stairs of our apartment. He was yelling at me and it was obvious that he was planning on hitting me. The husband of our friends ran up the stairs after Ed because he was afraid of what was going to happen. He pulled Ed off of me and asked him to go downstairs with him. Thanks to our friend, I did not receive a beating at that particular time. It was so embarrassing for me and our friends to witness scenes like this. I was more worried about being embarrassed, both for myself and for Ed, than I was about getting beaten. Again, this is probably because I had been beaten so often as a child and I was somewhat used to it.

Another time that I was embarrassed was again at the apartment in San Antonio. We were having a party, as we were prone to do about two to three times a month on the weekends. Our apartment was filled with people, and at some point, Ed got angry about something. He called me into our bedroom, saying that he had to tell me something. He then proceeded to beat me for about 15-20 minutes. One of our friends asked all of our guests to go home so that by the time I had gotten myself together and came out of the bedroom, all of our guests were gone. I felt terrible. I had company at our home, and not only did I get a beating with people there, the party ended during it and all of our friends had just left. I was at my wits' end, and at that time, did not know what to do about what was going on. I could not think straight and I was living minute by minute.

As anyone who has learned about the violence cycle understands, first comes the abuse. Then your partner is sorry, begs for your forgiveness, and often tries to follow that up with "love-making." They believe that if they can get you to have sexual relations with them, then you have forgiven them. What the abuser does not realize is that due to the abuse, the last thing you want to do with them is engage in sexual relations. You give in to them because you are afraid of retaliation if you do not have relations with them. In time, because your relationship has this major issue, you don't want to have *any* relations with them. I always felt that men wanted sex no matter what was going on in the relationship. For women, if there are problems of a dire nature (as were mine), we do not want to have relations with our partners at all.

Another issue that we had in our marriage that started when we moved to San Antonio was Ed always being out with his friends. He was in San Antonio for advanced lab technician school and ran into some guys that he had attended basic lab technician school with. His school was in the morning and he was usually done by 12:30 P.M. My school was in the afternoon into the evening—I was attending the basic lab technician school. He used the time I was in school to hang out with his guy friends for long hours. Many times, when it was time to come get me, he was many hours late.

There were many times, especially on the weekends, that Ed would go out with his guy friends and I would not see him for hours. Since we had only one car at that time, it would leave me stranded in our apartment. He never called to see if I was alright, nor did he call to let me know when he would be home. There were times when he left in the morning and I would not see him until two or three the next morning. It was very unsettling and it felt extremely disrespectful to be treated this way. Many times when he finally made it home, he was either high or had been drinking. I did not dare say anything about it, though, for fear that I would receive a beating if I did.

I realized when we hit the three-year mark of our marriage that things were probably not going to change. I still had hopes that they would, but was trying to be realistic. Ed had talked about having children many times before. I was holding off because I was still young and the marriage was in so much trouble. Around this time, I decided that I wanted to have a child. Ed wanted them so badly and I felt ready. Even though we were still having problems, we decided I would go off the birth control pill I was taking. I thought that maybe a child would help our situation. Later, I realized how silly those thoughts were.

Three months after going off the pill, I conceived. Ed and I were ecstatic. We were both so excited that we were having a child and I held high hopes that things would settle down now. I believed that Ed did not know what set him off when he abused me or why he was doing it. Maybe now that we had a child coming, he could control himself better? I am not sure what I was thinking, but I was happy and chose to focus on my pregnancy and the child that was on the way. I threw myself into my prenatal care and tried hard to eat as healthy as possible. I was about 120 pounds at that time and carefully watched my weight as the pregnancy progressed.

Since I was now pregnant, it seemed that Ed had slowed down on the abuse. He did not stop abusing me, but for the first six or seven months into the pregnancy, it was mostly emotional and verbal abuse. The physical abuse had slowed greatly. As my belly was growing and I was getting further along in the pregnancy, I started worrying about the physical abuse starting up again. Earlier, I mentioned that sometimes, he kicked me out of the car and made me walk home when he got mad. Well, since at this time we still had only one car, if he was not there to pick me up after work, I also had to walk home then.

I remember one day, after work, Ed did not show up to pick me up. It was five P.M. when I got off of work at the hospital. There were many times that he was late before, but he would come eventually. This time he did not. I waited 30 minutes for him to show up, and he never showed up. I started walking to our townhome, which was about two miles down the road. I was about seven to eight months pregnant by this time and it was extremely hot that day. It was August in San Antonio—summertime. The humidity was high there year-round.

I remember thinking that due to the heat and the humidity, I did not want to walk home. But I was tired of waiting, so I started to walk. I figured if he got to the hospital and I was not there, he would drive down the street and pick me up when he saw me walking. I got home at seven that night and went upstairs to lie down for a few minutes. Not only was it hot and humid, but I had a pretty good-sized belly by then. I was exhausted from the walk, so I rested for about 10-15 minutes. Then he ran through the door, yelling my name. I told him I was up in bed, and he proceeded to come upstairs. He was upset that I did not wait for him and that I walked home. I was shocked because it had been over two hours since he was supposed to have picked me up from work.

He started screaming at me, so to get away from him, I started going downstairs to our living room. He followed me as I was walking down the stairs and was trying to kick me. I ran faster down the stairs. When he could not connect his feet to my body, he pushed me down the stairs. I was worried about falling down the stairs at this stage in my pregnancy and was glad that there were only a few more steps to go when I fell. Of course, I was thinking more about the baby's safety than mine. I was shocked that he was so angry at me for walking home. What did he expect? Was I supposed to wait two hours for him to show up at the hospital to pick me up? I was tired, and even though I did not want to walk two miles in the heat and humidity to get home, I needed to get home.

So, the abuse had slowed while I was pregnant, but my fears had come true. He finally hit me while I was pregnant. I remembered feeling hugely disappointed that not even my being pregnant with his child—that he was so excited about—would stop him from trying to hurt me physically. My being pregnant did not stop his being out all the time, either. I remember one incident during my ninth month of pregnancy. He was hanging out with his friends as usual, and instead of being out from morning until two or three the next morning, this time he stayed out all night. I had no idea of where he was, and we did not have cell phones back then. It had been about 30 hours since he had left the house and I had received no calls from him. I was getting very concerned about his well-being.

The worst part of Ed being gone all this time is that we still had only one car. My coworkers were throwing a baby shower for me and I had to get there. I had told him the day before to please be home at a specific time so that I could get to the baby shower. About an hour before the baby shower was to start, I had to contact a neighbor to get a ride. He came over to our place and picked me up. We were driving down the road, not too long after we had left my home, and we had an accident. This friend did not tell me that he was having trouble with his brakes.

We were turning a corner and his brakes were not working correctly. We ended up crashing into a chain link fence, with the fence wrapping around the front of his car. I was in the front passenger seat. The neighbors all came out from around the area where we had crashed. Our friend, of course, was very upset because I was in my ninth month of pregnancy. Someone called the police, and soon there were officers on the scene. I was scared, but I felt fine and I just wanted to get to my baby shower. I did not want to be late, nor did I want people to know that my husband had not been home in over 24 hours. I was especially upset that my husband could not even be home to make sure I got to my baby shower. I felt that this was a special occasion, so I felt especially let down that he had not made it home—nor did he even care that I made it there.

Once we had established that I was not injured and I was not going into labor, another friend met me at the accident and gave me a ride to my shower. It was inconceivable to me that I would have to go through all of this trouble to get to my baby shower. It was further upsetting to me that Ed possibly did not come home on purpose and he intended to sabotage me getting to my shower. I was floored. I never thought that he would go this far to hurt me. I felt it was his fault I got into the accident and that our child had been endangered. If he had been at home as he was supposed to, none of this would have happened.

I made it to the shower and remember feeling blessed that I had good friends to not only help me get to the shower but to throw the shower for me. I tried to focus on the positive emotions and the fun of the event without trying to think about the hell I went through to get there. I was touched by all the people who showed up for the event and their kindness towards me. I knew that I should enjoy the time that I was having because when I got home, the drama would surely start. I couldn't imagine why Ed would have stayed out all night and into the next day. I also could not understand why, since the shower did not start until five P.M., he couldn't have honored my request to be home to take me to the shower.

The drama would continue. Ed came with me to Lamaze classes as my support system and also to learn what to expect when it came time for our baby to be born. It still did not prepare him, and I was grateful that I had a midwife in attendance when I finally went into labor. I went past my due date by about ten days. When I finally went into labor, I went to the hospital to give birth. The doctor thought it was early labor and sent me back home. We had already set up a date a few days after that to be induced if I did not go into labor before then. The inducement date was two weeks after the due date. I went back home with the instructions to take a warm bath, and if the contractions slowed, I was probably in false labor. I went home, took a warm bath, had a glass of wine, and played some cards. I felt as if the labor slowed after all that, and so I went to bed.

Ed got up early in the morning to go to school. I told him that I was feeling the pains come back, but they were not regular. I was not going into the hospital unless they were regular because I did not want to be sent home again. He went off to class, and I tried to go back to sleep after eating a bowl of cereal first. The pains got worse and worse, with me screaming many times through them. I was by myself, and even though Ed told me to call the school at any time if I wanted to go to the hospital, I was determined to make sure I truly was in labor.

By the time Ed came home after school at 12:30 P.M., I was worn out. I was perspiring heavily and begging him to take me to the hospital. I think he came home right from school for once because he knew I might be in labor. We went right to the hospital, and I believe I was in active labor by the time we got there. I knew then that they were not going to send me home this time. My midwife met us up there and they prepared me for delivery. When I was going through the worst part, I was trying to do my breathing correctly. Instead of breathing with me (as we had learned in Lamaze), Ed was screaming at me, "Breathe!" I have to say I was not surprised at his response.

I was thankful the midwife was there with me and was able to calm me down and help me with my breathing. When it came time to give birth, we were surprised at how large our son's head was. They did not do an episiotomy, so due to the largeness of my firstborn's head, I tore from "front to back." It was painful, but I was so happy to finally have my son out into this world and in my arms. Amidst all the challenges I was enduring, the birth of my son was a happy time for me. I was so excited to finally be a mother and to experience the birthing process. My son was long, skinny, and had a large-boned head. Once he was out, everything else went smoothly.

I stayed in the hospital for a week, healing from my tears and feeding my son. I picked him up from the nursery often and was so happy to care for him. I felt that no matter what happened between his father and me, I was going to focus on taking care of our son. I was so honored to be a mother. I spent all of my waking hours taking care of our newborn son. I was on active duty in the army at the time and had been given the last month of pregnancy off. Since I was almost two weeks late, I had about six weeks before Nathaniel was born. After the baby was born, the army gave me six more weeks off for the care of a newborn. So, I had a total of three months off for the birth of our son. I was happy to be able to be home to take care of him full-time for a little while.

As Nathaniel got a little older, we decided to buy a house on the outskirts of San Antonio. It was in a small town called Converse that had a small population and a police department of three men. I was so excited to have my first house, as well as room for our child. It was a three-bedroom house with two bathrooms. It had a large kitchen and living room with a beautiful fireplace. It was a brand-new home and we were its first owners. This new home was located about 20 minutes away from the base, and I felt that maybe since we were farther from the base, Ed would be at home more often.

It slowed his running around a bit but did not stop it entirely. He still was out for hours at a time and I received no calls. We finally bought a small, used car so that I would not be stranded by myself with a baby if he was gone for a long time. I was worried that if I had to get our son to the hospital in an emergency or go to any appointments for him, I would not be able to get there. So it was a relief to finally have a second car. Ed was not home very much, and when I asked him to take care of our son, it was "babysitting" to him. I never understood how you can "babysit" your child. As a mother, I would never say that I am babysitting my son, and so I was surprised to hear him say that to one of his friends.

I went back to work and continued to care for our son while at home. We had a great sitter taking care of him when we were at work. I felt like a single parent most of the time, though, because Ed still was gone quite a bit. I took care of the bills, the home, and the child. The abuse continued but was not as often. I think the reason for this was that Ed was not at home enough to do so. After graduating from advanced lab technician school, he was assigned as a drill sergeant for medic training at Fort Sam Houston. He was working some long hours and still trying to be out with his friends, hanging out at home or at the club for a few drinks.

The abuse was still ongoing, but it was less in terms of severity. I started feeling as if I was a single parent since I seemed to be taking care of everything. I dropped our son at daycare and picked him up also. The only thing that Ed was bringing into the home was additional income. I started thinking about asking for a divorce. There was not much relationship left between us and I felt as if I was doing all of the work inside the home and caring for Nathaniel.

There were times that after our son turned one (and was walking), he would react to his father's yelling and screaming. Many times when Ed said my name in a certain tone of voice, our son would run to his room crying from the fear of what was about to happen. I felt that he did not understand what was happening, but that specific tone of his dad's voice was familiar to him and meant something bad was about to transpire. Seeing that started affecting me, and I started thinking about the promise I made to myself when I left my parent's home. Since I had been brought up in an abusive environment, I had promised myself that my children would never come up the same way. If I was not smart enough to leave for my safety, now that I had a child, I had to put his needs and environment first.

It was around this time that we decided to have a large party in our home that was 20 minutes from the base. One of the girls in Ed's class had befriended me. I asked her if she wanted to help me with the party, and she said yes. She also volunteered to stay the night in our guest room and help me clean up in the morning. Since our home was a bit of a distance away from the base and the majority of the people attending did not have cars, I had to take some of our guests home after the party. The party went well, and I noticed that my husband was even drinking with others at the party. I left him and my friend to clean up a bit while I drove a bunch of people back to the barracks. It was 20 minutes one way, so I was gone for about 45 minutes.

When I unlocked the front door of the house I heard a whisper coming from the guest room: "It's Bobbi." I went straight to the guest room and found my husband and my friend in bed together. I was in shock. I remember thinking it was a good thing I didn't own a gun. I did not know what to do. As you can understand, I was not trying to figure the whole "how it happened" out in my mind. I was reeling from finding them together.

I went to my bedroom and just sat there in shock. I asked my husband to leave the home and not come back until the next day. I went to talk to my "friend" and asked her what happened. She made up a story that did not match the way that I found them. I took her back to the barracks and went home. Ed was back by then and tried to explain things to me. I did not know what to believe.

It took me a few days to sort through all of my thoughts. I was due to go home to New York for the Christmas holidays with my son and Ed. I decided to take my son and have Ed stay behind. I had talked things over with some good friends of mine and decided that this girl was lying. They had had consensual sex and I needed to get away on vacation to think over whether I was going to stay with Ed or divorce him. As I said earlier, I did not want a divorce, but at that point, Ed had now cheated on me in my own home. This was on top of the years of abuse from him. Also, I was starting to be concerned with our son's welfare. I was worried about his fears from seeing and hearing the abuse of his mother at his father's hands. He never was angry or violent with our son, thankfully, but the effects were real all the same.

I went home to my family for Christmas and allowed Ed to stay in the home. I was going to ask him to leave for us to be separated but wanted to think about things a bit more. He stayed in San Antonio while I went east. We had been separated the year before for a short time and I had him move into the barracks. This separation happened before we had our son and before we had bought this home. I felt that if we separated again, it would most definitely lead to a divorce this time. I wanted to be 100% sure that this was the only answer for us. While I was away, Ed called me every day and also cleaned our home from top to bottom. He was hoping that I would allow us to work this out and that I would not make him leave when I returned.

When I got home, I had decided for us to be separated again. I told him that he needed to move back into the barracks and that if he was willing to go to counseling, we would try to work things out. I needed him to be away from me for the time being because I was on emotional overload—it was all too much for me. In addition, I was starting to see that the environment in which we raised our son was starting to visibly affect him. Ed moved back into the barracks and we began another separation.

A little while later, after seeking some counseling of my own and consulting with a lawyer, I decided I wanted a divorce. I thought that if I was not smart enough to get out of this abusive situation for myself and my safety, I at least had to be a responsible parent and do it for my son. I asked Ed to meet with me outside of the barracks at the end of the work day. I was working in the hospital at the time as a lab technician, so I had on an all-white uniform. We met outside of the barracks in our van. I proceeded to tell him that I wanted a divorce. When he heard that, he got very upset with me and backhanded me in the mouth with his right fist. I proceeded to start bleeding, as he had cut open my lips quite a bit. The blood got all over the front of my uniform. I jumped out of the van immediately and went into the barracks to call the military police (since we were on base).

The MPs came and wanted to take me down to the station to file a report. I asked them if we could go pick up our son from the base daycare first. They took me over there, we picked him up, and then we went to the MP station. I was asked to write up a complaint against my husband while I was trying to watch my toddler. After I finished writing up my complaint, I was talking to another sergeant and Nathaniel fell off of the chair. I picked him up and comforted him, not knowing that he had busted his lip open. I removed him from my shoulder and felt a wet spot. I looked down and saw a large circle of blood. I could not believe it; we both had busted lips. Mine were worse than his, but it made me mad all over again.

When we were done, the MP took me back to my car. I drove home and put my son to bed. I called the local police department and informed them that the military police from Fort Sam Houston were looking for Ed. I gave them a summary of what had happened and they let me know if he were to show up at my door that I was to call them right away. Sure enough, a few minutes later, Ed showed up and wanted me to let him into the house. He had a dozen roses in his hand—I saw them through the peephole. This is part of the violence cycle that I was not aware of and would later learn about. I did not let him in but called the local police instead. They showed up and escorted him back to the MP station on base.

The MPs talked to Ed for a while and told him they would investigate my charges. I am not sure what there was to investigate, the evidence was obvious! A week or so later, Ed called me and said that his commanding officer wanted to talk to me. He was up for a promotion and he told me that he did not want me to go to talk to his CO. If I did go in, Ed told me that I had better lie for him. He had told his CO that I was upset with him and I had made the charges up; something along the lines of "a woman scorned." I was afraid to go in and talk to him, and I was not going to lie to protect him. I did not know it at the time, but because I did not go in and talk to his CO, the charges of assault were dropped against Ed.

I was in shock that this happened. Many times I had called the police when Ed had beaten me only to not file charges because I was afraid if they arrested him, he would not come home alive. I finally had enough and filed charges, and they were dropped. I was devastated and felt as if no one cared about protecting me or helping me in any way. I proceeded to file for divorce and had to wait about three to four months for it to be final. I still was very much in love with my husband, but I could not see any way out of this dangerous life with him except divorce. Even though I had every reason to get a divorce, I still struggled with whether it was a Christian thing to do or not. I felt in my heart, though, that God wouldn't want me or my son to be in a dangerous situation where we were constantly at risk.

Several times during our separation, Ed came by to see me under the pretense of seeing his son. We sold the house and I moved into an apartment after we parted. Despite this, I still lived in constant fear that he would attack me when I was outside of my home. The times that he came by and I would not let him in, he would bang on my windows and doors trying to get me to let him in. I would be crying and very scared about what would happen if I did. I was also in fear that he would break down the door and hurt me. There were a few times that I did let him in because I believed he wanted to see his son. He would visit with him for a few minutes, and then after he went to bed, he would want to talk to me. He would want to be intimate with me, and I would refuse him. As this was in the late 1970s, the belief was that it didn't matter if I was willing or not—since I was his wife, I "owed it to him."

This was just another way I felt abused. The bottom line is that I didn't have a voice. Many people did not believe me when I discussed what was going on, and I had no control over what was going on in my adult life. It was just an extension of my mother's control, but now it was my husband—Ed. Thankfully, things have changed and a woman can complain about abuses, be heard, and the man be prosecuted. I know that many abuses still go on and the justice system still has a long way to go, but things have gotten somewhat better as of today.

We were finally divorced in August of 1979 after almost five years of marriage. I decided to move outside of the state to Colorado. I had some friends there that I had previously visited, plus, I loved it there. So after my divorce was final, I left active duty, moved to Colorado, and joined the Reserves there. I lived in Colorado for over 31 years. Even though I knew that I had to leave San Antonio and get far away from Ed to have peace in my life, it was still hard to leave him. I had been in love with him for almost seven years—he was my first true love. I know it is hard to understand how you can love someone who hurts you so drastically, but you can.

You see their behavior as separate from your relationship at times. Deep down inside, I knew that Ed loved me deeply in some way. His actions said otherwise, and it was difficult to remember that he still loved me when he was beating me. If other issues in our marriage did not involve me and my son being in danger, I would have stayed and tried to work it out. Ed never wanted me to leave; he thought I should stay and try harder. He never understood why I left or how strongly I felt that I had to protect our son from being in that environment.

For about two years after I left Ed and moved to Colorado, I had a hard time disconnecting from him. I would often talk on the phone with him, and I felt like he had a hold on me somehow. It took a while for me to start dating after all of that happened. Even when I started seeing other people, I was still talking to Ed. There was an unhealthy codependency in our relationship and it took a long time for me to get healthy. I had to go into counseling for several years to learn that what happened in my childhood and my marriage was not my fault. I learned about the violence cycle that my ex-husband followed to the letter. My mother never used that cycle because most times she did not regret her abuse or try to make it up to us. I would mostly participate in individual counseling, but I did engage in group therapy for about six months before I felt I was strong enough to never let another person hit me or emotionally abuse me ever again.

25 years later, I would finally see Ed again and we would finally sit down face to face and discuss what happened. Not everyone will get that opportunity. I am blessed that I did so that I could get some closure after a long period. Ed and I talked for hours about what we felt happened, and what we took away from that relationship. I let him know the paths that I had to take to regain myself and the paths I had to go down to raise our son. He had not seen his son since he was about two years old, and would not see him until he was 31 years old. I want to be clear that Ed is not the same person today. He has changed and grown. We have made peace with each other. Not everyone does the work and tries to

do better, but we did. Ed did change. To this day, he will text me to say hello now and then. I have always left the door open to him to have a relationship with our son. As long as the situation was safe and made Nathaniel comfortable, Ed was welcome to visit.

I brought Nathaniel with me to attend his grandmother's funeral. It was a huge loss to me and my son to lose Ed's mom. Going to the funeral and seeing all of Ed's family after about 14 years was healing for us all. Ed was able to tell his son that he had always loved him even though he was not there for him for all those years. They are now trying to build a relationship and make up for some of the lost time. You can never make it all up, but they now have a chance to make new memories and to get to know each other as men. It is never too late to reunite with a family member and try to get to know them again. I feel it is important that you get to know your relatives when they have been out of your life for many years. Whenever there is a possibility to do so, it is a vital piece of the puzzle in a thorough understanding of who you are and what you are about. As I finish up this book for publishing, Nathaniel is staying with one of Ed's sisters. He has gotten some time to know that side of the family. I am truly glad that time, forgiveness, and communication can heal most things.

In closing, I know that many people who are being abused now cannot see a way out. There is *always* a way out. Sometimes it takes great planning and time. Many places and agencies can assist you with getting out. Do not feel as if you can never leave or there is no other life out there for you. No matter how many mistakes we make, no one deserves to be abused physically, mentally, verbally, or emotionally. Most abuse is about control, and the person trying to control you will never let you be an individual. If there are children involved, there is even more of a reason to get out.

I was raised in an abusive home. When I had children, there were times that I feared that my discipline could have possibly gone over the line. Whenever that happens or it looks as if it is a possibility it can happen, get help! There are many places you can go for counseling. A lot of counseling is on a sliding scale, so please do not let money or lack of money deter you from getting the help you or your family needs. I do not believe my son remembers the abuse that his father did to me, but he has other subconscious things that I needed to help him with through counseling. Do whatever it takes to get out of the situation, and get help for yourself and your children.

Remember that any time in life that we have these hurts and pains, we need to give ourselves the proper time to grieve. Different hurts need different types and periods of grief. Deep hurts take the longest amount of time to get over. There will be periods of anger, hurt, doubts, and sorrow. They can happen separately or at the same time. Give yourself the time and space to go through it all. Do not get involved in new relationships until you are over a good part of the grief. It is not worth it to take baggage with you into a new relationship when relationships are hard enough to work out on their own. Too many times, people don't give themselves enough time to grieve thoroughly and rush into new relationships because they cannot handle being alone. Many times, being alone is what is needed to get healthy. When you can be alone living a full and emotionally healthy life, then you will be ready to be in a relationship whenever it comes along. If you can be whole by yourself, then you can be a good half of a partnership.

Many people stay in abusive situations because they feel that they cannot support themselves. This is no reason to stay. By staying, you are creating more hardships for yourself and your children. You are causing more damage that will take longer to heal. There are many agencies out there to help you, along with shelters. Make use of all of the various groups out there to ensure that you get out, stay out, and get emotionally healthy. Unless we get emotionally healthy, we will continue to attract people that will hurt us. It can be a long process, but no matter what, it will always be worth it. Everyone deserves to be loved, appreciated and cared for. First, we must love ourselves and appreciate who God made us. We have to respect ourselves before others will respect us. Only then will we be able to love and respect someone else properly. Remember, we teach others how to treat us!

Chapter Five
Post-Abortion Syndrome

This is a very difficult chapter for me to write. I have to write this because there are way too many women out there who are hurting from having abortions and not being able to forgive themselves. Having an abortion can cause physical problems, emotional problems, and psychological problems. There have been millions of children killed every year through women having abortions and all of us are paying a huge price for this. Not only are the women having the abortion paying a price, but we as a society are paying a price. It is no wonder that since we have no regard for the life of an unborn child, we in turn have no regard for life at all. Why do we have so many people in our society who have no problem with killing others?

The respect and importance of human life are severely lacking in many of our people today – especially our youth. First let me give you some cold, hard statistics.

Post-Abortion Syndrome is REAL, I feel! Neither the medical community nor the psychological community recognize this syndrome and therefore does not give any validity to it. The millions of women who have had abortions, do give this syndrome some validity. They have lived through the lasting emotional and psychological aftereffects of having an abortion. Many know that something is wrong in their life, but cannot understand what that is.

Let us first talk about forgiveness. As a Christian who believes that Jesus died on the cross so that we may be forgiven of our sins - the second we ask for forgiveness - we get it from God. The hardest part of forgiveness for an abortion is forgiving ourselves. That takes many years. No matter the reason we went and had the abortion performed, there is an emptiness inside of us after the procedure is done.

Many women, (back in the days when I had mine), did not realize at that time that they were killing a child. I apologize for being honest and blunt, but for this subject matter, I feel it is necessary. I went to Planned Parenthood Clinics and received lots of information before considering having an abortion. At that time, I was told that I could not have an abortion until I was at least eight weeks along. I was also told, at eight weeks and beyond, that my embryo was not a child, but it was a mass of cells.

I don't know if they knew at that time that this was not true, or found out later. I believe that we have come far enough in our technology approximately 30 years ago to know the truth. I also have to believe that the medical community that was part of performing this procedure – removing the embryo with a vacuum, had to see that the parts that came out were formed as an early child and not a mass of cells.

Regardless, we do know the truth now and I believe it is murder. Just because the embryo is not fully developed and cannot live outside of the womb at 8-16 weeks, does not make it any less a child. Even before I found out the truth, I felt empty for many years after my procedure. There are many women out there who feel the same way. It affects every part of our lives- family, further pregnancies, our work – every area. Many of us do not realize how deeply we feel this emptiness and what not forgiving ourselves does to us.

Spiritually speaking, I believe that all children who lose their lives in abortions, miscarriages, or death of any kind, are in heaven. They are waiting up there for their mothers and when and if their mothers come to heaven after they die, they will recognize us. I believe this from the bottom of my heart, and it helps me to forgive myself for what I now know I have done. I look forward to the day that I die and go to heaven and see my other children. Many people in my life have passed on before me and while I am looking forward to seeing them, my children are who I want to see the most.

I have, for many years, struggled with forgiveness of myself in this matter. I believe God forgave me the second I asked for it, but for me to forgive myself, it has taken me many years. I also have realized that when, after all those years, I thought I finally had thoroughly forgiven myself, I had not. There was still a root deep inside my heart that needed the surgery of God to be removed totally.

I went to a ladies' conference given by a wonderful, gifted woman of God in my church. I had attended her conference once before, 4 years prior, and felt that many things had been dealt with then. In discussing with her about writing this book, she suggested that I attend another conference – to make sure that some of my deep hurts and issues were dealt with.

During that 3-day weekend conference, God spoke to this woman that out of the 10 women that were there, ALL of them had lost children through abortion or miscarriage. We had a ceremony that helped us recognize and deal with any deep pain and non-forgiveness that was still there. The next day we held a memorial service for our children. Without going into detail, due to the confidential nature and respecting the privacy of the women attending this conference with me, suffice it to say that I had not gotten all of the "root" out.

Through our exercises, I was able to finally finish forgiving myself along with recognizing the full extent of what this had meant in my life. I had blocked out some events surrounding my abortions, and God was revealing much to me. I was able to finish forgiving myself and finish getting the "root" out of my heart. God was able to heal me once and for all which allowed me to close that chapter in my life. God showed me that many women were suffering from this type of pain and non-forgiveness.

Through this exercise and research after, I was strongly led to write about this subject in my book. My main purpose in writing this book is to help other women with real issues and challenges that I have survived. I want to help women deal with these hard issues and allow God to help them work through these issues, not around them. There are a lot of resources for women who are suffering from this challenge and there is also lots of help for them.

It has taken most of 40 years now to finish this process of forgiving myself, getting the rest of the roots out, and truly moving forward from this pain and suffering. I want to encourage any woman or man who has a woman in their life that has gone through an abortion, to reach out and get help. Do the research and learn about this subject matter. In addition, reach out and ask for help. First, ask God to forgive you, and then work on forgiving yourself. It will make a huge difference in your life and allow you to move towards total healing of your mind, emotions, and possibly your body. Things that we hold deep inside us affect us in our physical bodies also.

Please remember that millions of women have gone through this, survived this, and have been able to forgive themselves. It is not easy! In the end, it will set you free. Once you are free, you will remain free from this pain and suffering regarding this issue. Do not ever allow Satan or anyone else to chastise you for this issue ever again. Do not believe the lies that he or anyone else will tell you. Believe only what the Word says – confess your sins and God will be gracious to forgive them. Once they are forgiven by Him and by you, do not ever take them on again. They are gone, and are as far as the "east is from the west".

I want to end by saying that being this transparent in my book is not easy. I know I should not feel any shame regarding this after all this time. I also know that God has forgiven me and I have forgiven myself. At this age, 68, it is way more important to help others than to worry about what people think of me. We ALL have things we have done in the past. Our past does not define our present except to show that we have changed, grown, and have been forgiven. My sole purpose for writing this book was to help others to heal and move on from trauma. This is the sole purpose that I believe God has asked me to be transparent, I am obeying Him so that I can help others! As mentioned in my introduction, it is my biggest passion in my life now. It is time to give back and to help others to walk through their challenges. Who better than someone who has suffered the same things? I understand others walking through these things because I have walked through them. God loves you! He will help you to walk through ALL things!

Chapter Six

MUSIC IS IN MY BLOOD

I HAVE ALWAYS KNOWN THAT MUSIC IS IMPORTANT TO ME, BUT never knew just how deep the roots were. Recently, God has begun to show me how it has been passed down from my grandmother to my mother and father, down through us kids, and down through my children – even to my grandchildren.

I just recently found out that my grandmother on my mother's side was a singer. I am not sure if she was a professional, but from what my mother remembers, Grandma Ethel was an outstanding singer. She passed that gift down to my mother, her daughter. My mother was gifted with an awesome mezzo-soprano voice from a young age. I have heard many stories of her doing solos and performing as she grew up. When it came time for her to go to college, she received a voice scholarship to go to Beaver College (now called Arcadia), located outside of Philadelphia, PA. She studied music for four years and has extremely fond memories of those years. She did many recitals during that time and showed me the pictures from that time, repeatedly. She would continue to sing all of her adult life, well into her 80s. It was only after getting Alzheimer's and not being able to remember the music, that she was forced to give it up. She sang in the Babylon Chorale for almost 50 years.

She was a paid soloist in many churches as I grew up. When she was singing, she seemed like a different person. For as long as I can remember, she was a member of the Music Lovers group on Long Island, New York. Music Lovers, every spring would sponsor talented young people and assist them with some scholarship monies to attend college. I remember attending many of these events with her as a young girl. One year, our whole Cranston family put on a concert for them. My dad played the piano, my oldest sister the cello, my oldest brother the trombone, my other oldest sister the flute, me the violin, my youngest sister the viola, my mother sang and my youngest brother (at the time about 10) conducted us all. It was a lot of fun and one of the few times we were on one accord.

My father played the piano and organ. I always found great joy in listening to him play throughout the years. He accompanied many of us kids growing up, as we all studied different instruments. He sacrificed money to give me private lessons for many years in the violin since he felt I was especially gifted. He and my mother spent many hours driving me to my private lessons, sometimes the distance being far. As mentioned in the chapter on my dad, as he grew older, he still played his organ. The last time I saw my dad alive, he played his keyboard for us. I took a picture of this and I still have it today. He always looked so peaceful and in a different world whenever he played – I know it always brought him great joy when he was playing.

From my mother and father, we all inherited that gift of music. All six of us children sang growing up along with playing an instrument. Music was an important part of our different classes in school back in those years. Today, art and music have been taken out of the curriculum for kids due to budget cuts. Back in the day, we all learned to read music and to understand the different components of music. I took private violin lessons for many years. I also played in the school orchestra and performed in many concerts. I played many solos in church along with competing in the New York competitions. In my high school years, I played in the Long Island Symphony for a few years. I remember thinking that it was strange for a handful of us teenagers to play with mostly (to me) much older people. We made beautiful music and at that time I did not appreciate the honor that was being bestowed on me.

From as young as I can remember, I and my siblings sang in the choir at our church. Our church had various choirs, broken down by age groups. I have always loved to sing, not realizing until many years later, that God has given me the gift of praise and worship. The Word says "Don't let the rocks cry out", and I have always chosen to let my instruments of praise cry out. Growing up in my dad's church, most of our music was hymns. I learned the beauty of hymns and they have a special place in my heart as part of our music history. I was later, in my teenage years, introduced to Gospel music. I was amazed when I first heard it. I was very blessed to be able to visit other churches in town to worship with my friends. The first time one of my friends invited me to come to their church, I was apprehensive. It was different from our church, but I found it very refreshing. I loved Gospel music immediately and to this day, it is a huge part of me and my praise for our Lord.

I remember thinking when I first heard the Gospel that it was a different type of worship than the hymns that I was used to singing. The singers seemed to be much more emotional and appeared to reach out to praise the Lord on a different level. I was enthralled with it and from those early years, I felt that I didn't think that I would ever be able to sing Gospel music. Little did I know that God would continue to have me going to different churches in my early adult years, and I would participate in singing Gospel music many years later.

I was a member of the Word of Life Christian Center in Lone Tree, Colorado. I was a member there for over 26 years and would end up raising all four of my children there. Soon after becoming a member there, I became involved in the Praise and Worship team. I quickly learned different types of Christian music including that old-fashioned type of Gospel, and Contemporary Praise music which includes sometimes singing refrains over and over. I was used to singing music while reading it from sheet music. I was trained all my childhood to read music and knew my harmony parts from that reference. I have a lower voice and mostly would sing the alto part of 4-part harmony. I have always had a strong voice and an ear for harmony.

Singing on the Word of Life Praise and Worship team for so many years, I had to learn to sing by ear. I had never done that before and it was uncomfortable in the beginning. While it was a challenge, I quickly learned that I was chosen by God to praise and usher in the spirit of worship. I was in awe of a new feeling in my spirit and soul that came when I sang in this "venue". I began to learn what it meant to truly Praise our Lord and worship Him and how it made me feel. It was like something was being released deep within me. I also felt led to teach that to young people. For many years, I taught children's choir along with working with our children's holiday presentations. These presentations were dramas with music and while they were trying at times due to many practices, costumes, and the normal working with children issues, they brought great joy to me.

I have been on the Praise and Worship team off and on for many years now. Our team at WOL released several CDs, under the direction of our pastor's son. It was awesome to see God work with him over the years. He went from being a young child in my kid's choir to now being an internationally known producer and composer of music. Watching him grow up and grow in his music, has been one of the experiences that shows me how mighty God can be. God gave him the gift of playing the piano while he was a teenager and it seemed very spontaneous. Then later in his teen years, he began writing music. I was always in awe of God moving in his life. He may have not yet had the maturity to deal with all of us and our different personalities, but he had the gifts and talent for music.

We started as members of Word of Life when Nathan was 9, Carrie was 3, and Chris 3 months old. Jonathan was born in the first few years of us attending there and all four grew up in a life of music. They heard music, mostly Christian, in our home. For a long period, I did not allow any secular music into our world while they were growing up. I know they heard it in other kid's homes, but I was determined that they would not be " poisoned" by secular music- the words and spirit of it. The kids were not happy about this, but since I was the mom and making the "rules", this was the way it was. I also did not allow them to go to all of the dances at school. I relaxed a bit as they got older, but mostly had Christian praise music and Gospel playing in our home and my car.

As my children grew, I began to learn that as important as music was to me, it became important to them. Even as a baby, I started to see my oldest son, Nathan, begin to respond to music. He was six months old, and there was some Michael Jackson music playing on the radio in our van. He started to move to music and was on the beat! A few years later, as he was talking better, he began to remember words to songs and began to sing. Soon after we joined Word of Life when he was 9, he began to sing in my kid's choir. He acted and sang in the productions that we put on back then.

A few years later, he competed in youth music at the yearly retreats for our youth groups. These retreats would be nearby with youth from many churches attending in the western region of the U.S. I stood in awe every year and watched him mature in the gift that God had blessed him with. The first time I heard him compete and sing "Mount Mariah ", I just cried. I recognized at that moment that he had been blessed with a special gift and it aroused something in me that I could not name at the time.

As Nathan got a few years older and was in high school, it became frustrating for the other kids competing in the yearly retreats. Nathan would always win and they began to wish for some reason that he would not be able to make it. I remember one year there was an awful blizzard. The competition was about an hour away. We were all meeting at the church and the Pastor had not yet decided whether the youth would be able to go due to the storm. One of our sister churches that was about 20 minutes from where we were located had been able to make the trip. They let us know that down south, where the competition was, it was not snowing. I was going to drive my minivan and the church was sending a large van with all of the teens that were going to sing in the competition.

Around the time the competition was getting ready to start down south, Pastor decided it was too dangerous to drive the church van. I let him know that I was going to still try to make it in my minivan. The snow had not let up, but living in Colorado for many years to this point, I was used to driving in blizzards. I was willing to take a risk because it was important to my son to be there. I heard later (and already knew it to be true), that many of the kids down at the competition were hoping that the group from our church would not be able to make it due to the storm. I did feel sympathetic to them; after all, they just wanted a shot at winning. Nathan singing alone, and with others doing duets, were always winning these competitions.

I asked Pastor if I could try to drive down. He said if I wanted to take the risk it was alright with him since I was taking my vehicle. He let me know that if I wanted any other kids from the youth group to ride down with me; I had to get permission from their parents. I called the parents and got permission for the 2-3 that came with us. The minivan seated 7 and I had my other 3 children. We proceeded to drive through that awful snowstorm, praying every mile we traveled. I remember seeing many cars in the ditches along the way that had driven off the road. The actual highway had about 5-6 inches of snow on top of it. The plows could not keep up with the heavy snowfall. It was white-out conditions and I could not see the road. I trusted God and drove very slowly, following someone else's tail lights; when I could see them. About 30 minutes into the trip, Nathan told me that he had to go to the bathroom and could not hold it any longer. His stomach was cramping up. I was scared to stop because I felt that I did not know where the side of the road was and that we might get stuck. He continued to complain of his stomach hurting, so I finally inched over to where I thought the side of the road was. He quickly got out and walked a few feet.

The snow was so thick that I told him to not go very far. First of all, no one could see him go to the bathroom, but I was truly worried that we would lose him out there. He had on a black suit so that at least I could see a bit of him after he walked a few feet. I was frantic that he would get soaked and possibly not be able to see the van to get back to it. He finally came back after a few very anxious minutes for me. Everyone in the van cheered and we slowly made our way back onto what I believed to be the road. Normally this trip takes about one hour. This time it was a two-hour trip for us. Once we got down to the town, it was not snowing much there. I found the church and we arrived at almost the end of the competition. I could see on the other kids' faces that they were disappointed that we made it. There were only a few more competitors left to perform. Nathan performed a duet with a friend and also did a solo. These two performances were the last two. My son and all of us who made that trip were happy that we had made it safely.

It wasn't about winning that made this victory sweet. It was about God protecting us and allowing us to make it there safely. I felt that Nathan and his partner had worked hard on their music and the goal was to perform. Even if Nathan hadn't won, I truly felt that the trip down to the competition was important for many reasons. Singing is something that Nathan cared about, a gift that God had blessed him with, and was something that brought great joy to him. He worked hard to honor that gift and performing brought him his reward for what he had put into it. The trip also taught him and the other kids that if we put our minds to something, and it is God's will to do so, we would be protected by Him. Life many times is like this snowstorm – you have to step out in faith. Even though you cannot see but a few feet in front of you, you must trust our Father to lead us down the path that He wants us to go. Our circumstances (the snowstorm) may not look very good, but God will see us through!

In Nathan's 10th and 11th grade years, Pastor prophesied over him that his calling was to minister to millions of people in music. He said he wasn't sure if it was in making an album, traveling abroad on the mission fields or here at home. I remember thinking, how awesome our God is! I knew He gave Nathan this awesome gift, and I was excited for him that God was going to use this to bless millions. It seemed at the time hard to believe, but I know my God is "able"! Nathan has not yet, at the time of this writing, fulfilled that calling. I know that God's Word does not come back "void" and that at some point he will. He has sung in groups in college and for quite a few weddings.

A few times before Nathan left for college, we sang before our congregation together. I felt so blessed every time that we did this, still in awe of his awesome gift from God. I remember the last time we sang together, as if it was yesterday, even though it was about 30 years ago. It was the last Sunday he would be home before leaving to attend college. I chose the song "Giving My Best" by the Brooklyn Tabernacle Choir. This song especially ministered to me because Nathan was growing up and leaving for college. I considered raising him as one of my best accomplishments, and I completed it with God by my side. Before we sang the song, I told the congregation that as Nathan was leaving for college, I was "giving my best" to the Lord. God gives us our children and with Him, we mold and raise them in the ways of the Lord. Once they go off to college and into adult life, we give them back to God. We sang the song and God anointed it. By the time we were done singing it, there was not a dry eye in the house, even the men were discreetly wiping tears from their eyes. It blessed me so much and is one of the most treasured memories of my life.

Nathan went to Stanford University and sang with two different Acapella groups. The first one was a very old and honored group called Fleet Street Singers. While he sang in that group the first two years of college, they were chosen to go to the collegiate National championship at the Lincoln Center in New York. It was a huge honor and even though they did not win the championship, they placed very highly in the competition. Along with the most awesome experience of competing was the opportunity for Nathan to be on television. I was surprised to learn and honored when I saw him and his group on the Today Show. That is a very popular morning news show that is on for a few hours every Monday through Friday and is filmed at Times Square in New York. I watched the show, feeling so blessed and honored by what God had bestowed on Nathan and our family. They sang several songs and Nathan was the lead singer. I felt so emotional watching him thinking that no matter what I had come through thus far; God had honored one of my children greatly. I cried and felt so proud of all that Nathan had accomplished so far.

After singing with that group for 2 years, Nathan chose to sing with Everyday People, another Acapella group at Stanford. He sang with them for three years, since he decided later to stay for his Master's degree. While he was singing with this group, he was part of many concerts and several CD projects. I saw him once when his group traveled nearby to Fort Collins, Colorado. I took the rest of my kids and stayed in a hotel there to see him perform. Every time Nathan sings, it fills me with awe and joy. He has been chosen to be given such a huge gift and one that means a lot to our heritage. His voice is so anointed that it brings tears to my eyes every time I hear him.

Another very special memory that involves my kids singing was when I lost my father in December 2000. I planned a memorial service to take place the day before Father's Day about 6 months after his death. The reason we had to wait is because one of my older sisters, Bonnie, lives in Japan. She had to be able to fly from Japan to New York for the service and also have a break from her school year – she taught English and music to the Japanese children. In planning the service, I wanted to give honor to how much music meant to Dad, so I had lots of music. My younger sister Claudia's two youngest girls were about 5 and 8 at the time. I had them do a special song along with sign language. It turned out so beautiful and touched everyone there. Also, a young woman, who had been ministered to by my Dad, sang. She attributed his kind heart to changing her life. She sang a song that she had written. It was so moving and meant a lot to us as a family.

I had Nathan, Carrie, and Christopher, my three oldest, sing "Thank You" by Ray Boltz. They had little time to practice together since Nathan was still away at college and had to come in from San Francisco to attend the service. This song epitomized my father. It spoke so eloquently about people that ministered to young children and as these children grew up and went to heaven, they thanked those people. It was so meaningful because my dad had such a caring heart and loved people so well. He ministered to many throughout his years here on earth and I am sure that when they get to heaven, they will say "thank you" to him. He was a hugely important person in my and my sibling's life and I will talk more about that in another chapter.

Christopher, my third child, as he was growing up was hugely involved in sports. He sang in my children's choir but never showed a large interest in music. I had him participate (for many years) in the choirs at school. When the kids were in 3rd grade or so, the schools introduced the Tonette to all of them. Music programs had been cut back due to budget over the years, so music wasn't as integral a part of their education as it was in my generation. He never chose to play an instrument in his younger years. In the spring of his junior year in high school, he started showing an interest in the guitar. A very good friend of his from church was very gifted in the instrument. Chris asked this young man to teach him to play. They had a few lessons together, and Chris picked it up very quickly. About 6 months later, Chris started to write songs. I was simply amazed and touched as he began to sing them for me.

In his senior year, he had written a few and was asked to perform at one of his High School concerts. I had not heard this one and was very moved when I heard him perform it. It was a story about a teenage girl who had become pregnant in high school. It talked about the struggles she went through as she chose to have the child and keep the baby. She was judged by her peers greatly as she struggled to stay in school throughout the pregnancy and after the baby was born. The song talked about forgiveness and love along with the lesson of her fellow students not being judgmental of her. It was so caring and deeply touched many in the audience. I remember thinking that I was again in awe of one of my kids' musical abilities and that I had a child who was writing music. That is something that my parents nor my siblings had never accomplished.

In church, while Chris was in high school, he joined our Praise and Worship team. I was singing on the team at the time and it was fun to have him in the group with me. He grew and matured as a singer further, being chosen to be one of our lead singers for the last few years until he went off to college. He sang a few specials, but mostly concentrated on writing his music and playing the guitar. We occasionally had concerts at church – talent shows- and he did perform in a few of those. I was amazed to see his gifting grow especially since I thought that he would be going on in sports into college with a football scholarship. I now know that I was wrong and God had some other things in store for him.

Chris went to college, Oral Roberts University, to get a degree in Business. He also got a minor in Music. Due to his minor in music, Chris studied a lot of music theory and other classes. He learned to play the piano in one of these classes and liked the guitar; he picked it up very quickly. It was as if he had been playing these two instruments as a youngster when most kids started with them. Oral Roberts University also has a ministry show on television and it has been airing for many years. It used to be called "The Hour of Healing" and then called "Something Good Tonight". I was surprised to learn that after only a semester of attending the University, he had been asked to audition for the TV Singers. They are a small group of about 6-7 singers that perform on the show, doing 2 worship songs at different spots in the show. He sang with the other singers and Richard Roberts, who with his wife Lindsey, was in charge of the show. Richard heard him and immediately let the others know that he wanted Chris in the group. I was very excited to hear this and again, in awe, another one of my children was going on in a major way with music in his life.

Chris went on to sing with this group being on television for three years. Soon after performing on the show, he started to date one of the other singers, Kelly. They would later get engaged and another year later would be married. God gave them a calling to write and sing music together along with leading worship teams later on. Chris had already written many songs by this time. Some had words and some didn't. They would go on to write over 40 songs, along with releasing a worship CD. Even though they both eventually graduated with business and marketing degrees, their minors in music were for many years the vocations that would most speak to their hearts.

In the past 12-15 years my youngest son, Jonathan has been starting to write music also. It was prophesied over him in his teen years by our Pastor, "that God would wake him up in the middle of the night and give him songs". He was instructed to have a pen and paper by his bed at all times. In addition, it was prophesied that he would "go forth with the word", and be a minister. I was in awe back then when I heard that and immediately thought of my father. Jon would go on to get a four-year Local Pastor degree at Oral Roberts University while running on the ORU track team.

Jon sang in many choirs growing up also, but never showed any interest in an instrument. In his high school years, he also sang in one of our Praise choirs at Word of Life. In addition, he was in our youth band, many times leading the songs. As he was attending Oral Roberts University, God led him to start leading worship in a startup church there on campus. In the last 6+ years, Jon has been living in China and teaching English. He has continued to sing and play his guitar, many times performing live.

My grandchildren now are carrying on the giftings of music. My oldest granddaughter, Elora, has tried her hand at playing the violin and also loves to sing. She has performed in some talent shows in the past few years. My 11-year-old grandson, Bennett is doing very well learning the piano and singing in his school's choir. Gemma, who is now 7, has an amazing voice and takes after her mother and my son. She is now studying the piano, picking it up quickly. She appears to have a passion for music also. She sings all the time. She showed signs before she was even one year old that she would have a very well-tuned ear for singing. My youngest grandchild, Azalea who is currently 5, loves to sing and dance.

It warms my heart to see that the heritage my parents and grandparents passed down to us, will continue to pass down through the generations to come. As we all continue to sing and play instruments, it ministers to our hearts and souls. Even though my heritage has lots of pain and suffering, God brings us through it all. He is using all the brokenness along with these awesome gifts to minister to many and it is such an honor. I thank God every day for our blessing and our callings. He has chosen us, regardless of our past. God is a good God and shows us so much mercy and grace. He died on the cross for our sins and forgives us easily. He knows the purposes for which He has chosen us! Even if we stray off of our chosen paths, we eventually come back and He works through us in miraculous ways.

Chapter Seven
Single Parenting

I was a single parent for 30-plus years. I have a lot to share to help other single parents. First, though, I want to address the fact that being a product of an abusive childhood had some ramifications on my parenting style. I learned in my childhood environment, that when under stress, you yell and at times strike out. Of course, when looking back there are things that we wish we did not do. In 20-20 hindsight, I wish I was calmer, more patient, less strict, and did not yell. It was a very stressful time and it was hard to take care of all 4 children mostly by myself. I worked an average of 60 hours per week most of my adulthood to provide for the kids.

My oldest son was almost two when I finally got divorced and moved away to Colorado. I only had him at this time but I was living without a partner for the first time. I decided to pick up a part-time job on top of the 40 hours I was already working. I was very stressed and overtired. One time I got really angry at Nathan, and I was instantly afraid. I felt that my mother was going to come out in me even though I promised myself that I would never let that happen. I did not react to that stress well.

After that, I realized I needed help to work through my childhood trauma and sought therapy. I am sad about this very stressful incident, but grateful it woke me up to my need for getting therapy and working through my childhood trauma. I recognized that becoming abusive, similar to how my mother was to us, might become a real problem. It has been said that statistically, this happens often. I was determined not to allow this to happen to me. I immediately sought out counseling. I was financially strained, but I was able to find a program at a University that was on a sliding scale. I was very appreciative that I could find this program, as I needed this counseling direly.

At this same time, I noticed that Nathan was exhibiting other behaviors of fear that I could not figure out where they came from. I believed him to be too young at 1.5 years to remember the abuse from his father to me. Subconsciously, maybe he did remember, and before he attended preschool or kindergarten, I was determined to get it all worked out. So, counseling was a viable and necessary option for us both.

As mentioned above, I unfortunately did a lot of yelling as a mom. Another learned behavior that was brought on by stress. When my children did not listen or willfully disobeyed, I yelled. I would come home so tired from working so much and of course, did not have much patience. I had a chore that was to be done daily before I got home. I wanted the kitchen sink to be empty. I asked my children over and over to please rinse their dirty dishes and put them in our dishwasher, which was right by the sink. I came home repeatedly to find dirty dishes in the sink. I could not understand why this simple task could not be completed. My children were teenagers at this time.

While this is just an example of what set me off often when I walked in the door, there were others. I finally realized that many of the times I yelled or disciplined my children I was angry. Unbeknownst to me I was also suffering from PTSD to some things that happened a few years earlier in the Army. We will talk about this in a later chapter. Needless to say, there had been trauma in my childhood, the military, and with my abusive ex-husband.

This was not healthy for me or my children. Unfortunately, when I had my oldest two children, ages 22 and 28, I was still learning. I was probably much stricter and made more mistakes with their disciplining than I did with the younger two. I was 31 and 34 when I had the younger two. I was more mature, learned more about parenting, and relaxed a bit more.

As time went on, I learned that when coming home, it was best to go to my room after speaking to my children. In their later years as children, I think they resented that too. It was my coping mechanism from working so much and being so exhausted. I did not want to take it out on them. I told them when I came out; I wanted those things that would have set me off, to be taken care of. Later on, I would learn different ways of disciplining, such as removing a TV show or taking away their phones for a bit.

I am sharing all of this with you to let you know that I made many mistakes as a single mom. The fact that there was no one to have my back to help me made things a lot worse. I believe because I was the only one, that the children pushed me more. They figured out if they did not listen to me, no one else would be able to back me up or discipline them. There was more disobedience due to this fact, along with them just being kids. It is very difficult to raise children alone.

Not only was discipline a huge issue, but providing for my children also. I had to work to provide, and many times since it was only me, I worked 2 jobs. This put a lot of pressure on me for daycare, getting the children to different schools, etc. It took a physical and mental drain on me. I also felt guilty over the limited amount of time spent with my children. I tried very hard to take them places and do lots of fun things with them to make up for it. I always felt upset that I did not have more time to just play with them and hang out together.

One of our fun family times together was having a Friday night pizza and movie night. We would all agree to a movie, or two and I would order pizza. It was a lot of fun and a great way to get some bonding time with my children. I know it did not make up for the amount of time I was out of the home working two jobs, going to school, being in the Reserves, etc. It did make the time we spent together valuable and I tried hard to make it fun.

One thing that a single mom or dad will feel is a lot of guilt for the amount of time they have to be away from their children. If there is any family around or close friends, they can ease this problem and some of the guilt. Friends are also invaluable to a single parent. I will go into more detail about the wonderful friends that God blessed me with in a later chapter. It is so hard to be in so many places at once and when working is necessary along with the many extra hours, a single parent needs all the help they can get. I was fortunate that Nathan was an older child when the others came along. Unfortunately for him, he was a huge helper to me raising the younger ones. He changed many diapers and got them dressed as much as me. Many times, he was enlisted as their sitter, which I am sure he was not happy about some of the times. I don't know how I would have made it if it were not for him. God knew what he was doing, giving me a responsible, older one to help out. I still felt bad that he had to help so much and many times I am sure he would have been happy to be doing something else. At that time I was doing whatever it took to survive and was not able to see things. Survival mode is a brutal way to live. It does not leave you a lot of time to contemplate or evaluate how things can be done better.

Other things that are difficult for a single parent are clothing, feeding, and housing your kids. Do not be ashamed or prideful when it comes to accepting help from others. God had to teach me humility. I did not want to let on that I was struggling. I did not want to ask for help but quickly learned that for my kids' benefit, I needed to. Do not be afraid to ask for help from any agencies that are out there. While I was working and in school, I was able to get temporary assistance with food stamps along with other government food assistance. My kids have "fond" memories of that block of cheese and peanut butter that was given to us. I remember the assistance of WIC. Women, Infants, and Children were a huge help to me with formula, infant cereal, and other young child necessities. Powder milk that I mixed with regular milk or made alone, was used a lot. My kids drank gallons of milk a day. They are still telling stories of powdered milk to this day.

Along with food, I took advantage of daycare assistance. I called my local Mile High to get a list of licensed daycare providers in my area. This could be a daycare center or a personal home daycare person. For the first two years of college, I had my daycare paid for by the government. It was a huge help. I wanted to get a degree to earn more money to make things easier for us financially. It was hard but worth it. I also had the GI Bill from being on active duty in the Army for 6 years, and that helped also. There is a lot of assistance out there. Do not be ashamed to use it, especially if you are working or in school. It is perfectly alright to get help, especially when you are helping yourself too.

Other single parents that you know are another huge resource. If you have other friends who are single parents, it would be great to make a network of sitters. This way maybe once a week or every other week, you can get a break and spend some time with friends or even by yourself. Be sure to take a break for you. I didn't learn this lesson until later on. One time, a counselor told me something that stuck with me. If I did not spend time alone to recharge, I would not be a good parent. I started doing small things, like taking a bubble bath after the kids went to bed. It made perfect sense, but we have a hard time seeing this while we are rushing around taking care of our kids. We are in the "zone" and are rushing around day in and day out, to provide and keep them well. My focus was on feeding, caring, and making sure they were happy, and I lost myself. I was always at the bottom of the list.

Many times while we are so busy being a mom or dad alone, we lose ourselves. I didn't know that I had another name besides "Mom". That is all I had time to focus on and to be. It was very important to get some alone time and to pamper myself. To realize that there is a "me" and not only a "mom" was so needed for me to recharge. If I couldn't take good care of myself, how could I take good care of my kids? There is a little girl inside every woman and a little boy inside every man. That little person is necessary to us being balanced and sometimes we need to take care of that little person inside us all.

While there was not much money left over after bills; a common struggle of single parenting, there are many things to do out in the community for free. The local zoo and museums have free days. The local library is another free resource. There are book readings, arts and crafts, and many activities geared toward children. Along with these, I feel it important that you instill the desire for reading in your children. This starts with you reading to them whenever possible. Then you will instill a love for books and learning. This will help them in school along with being a huge advantage for them if they head on to college. In the newspaper and online are activities in the community for families.

Make use of all that is out there for you. I would make even a trip to the grocery store an adventure. At times, when our old cars were on the blink, we would have to take the local buses to the stores and other events. Make an adventure out of everything, instead of focusing on the car being broken down.

Another area that is important for a single parent is to teach their kids how to manage money. Since the kids accompanied me to many appointments and errands, they were around many times when I made financial decisions. There are banks in your community that have young people's checking accounts. They can open a checking account, put a little bit of money in (maybe an allowance), and be able to learn how to use a debit card or write a check. You would be on their account, have to sign their check, and monitor all usage. This is an excellent way to teach them how to manage money. When my kids were teenagers, I also took them along when I bought a car. I taught them how to use the Kelly Blue Book to find out the value of a car and how to "wheel and deal" when it came to the dealerships. These lessons are invaluable to prepare them to be able to successfully take care of themselves as an adult.

One other area I want to discuss that is very important for single parents. While your child may have their other parent around, many times they do not. As a single mom, two out of my four kids did not have their father around at all. One had him around occasionally, and the youngest had his dad around regularly. There are organizations like Big Brother, and Big Sister that can help. They screen thoroughly the candidates before they spend time with your child. Whatever the "missing" parent's sex is, they can learn to have a role model for them to see what a good adult of that sex acts like. Another group could be your church. Our church had men's day and for those sons whose dads were not around, the single men "adopted" a boy for that day and did the events with them. We were very blessed that a young man stepped up with my middle son and was eventually there also for my youngest son. This person was very instrumental in our lives in being an outstanding man to role model what a good man looks like and acts like. As they became teenagers, he taught them to drive, about finances, business, and the characteristics of a great person. To this day, this awesome man is still in their lives and gives them advice on relationships, business, and life in general.

Another way to have good role models in your kids' lives is to make sure they spend time around a healthy married couple. They need to see that there are relationships out there that, while not perfect, are good and they work together to make it work. For my three sons and my daughter, it was invaluable to have them spend time around my best friend's husband. Whatever is lacking in their immediate home, can be modeled and fulfilled in other relationships. While there are many single-parent homes, your children must see and live around others who will fill that "void" and lessons that are healthy to learn.

I have mentioned elsewhere in the chapter, "Breaking Up is hard to do", but I want to mention it again because it is important. Dating while a single parent is very tricky. It is wise to keep any relationship away from your children until you are sure that this person is going to be with you in a committed relationship and there is a strong possibility that it may lead to marriage. It is tough enough for your children to have only one parent and wish there was someone else, but to bring others around and they don't last, it can be devastating to them. I spent many years not dating, because of time and focus. I was busy working two jobs, in school, Reserves, and church, and spending time with my children. I prayed that if "the one" would come along during this time, we would be friends first. I would not bring that person around my children until we were in a committed relationship. I also prayed at the beginning of a relationship, that if this person was not the "one", the Lord would remove him from my life. He does answer prayers, so be ready for the answer. I did long for companionship, but since I had some amazing long-term girlfriend relationships, I did not get lonely. It is much more important with how your children will suffer if you don't handle this carefully than you being with someone. It is a pretty sticky situation and should be handled with care. I know that you desire companionship with the opposite sex, but as a single parent, your priority is always your children. Pray about each person that comes into your life and rely on God's knowledge for your wisdom and discernment.

Lastly, I want to remind you that having children is a blessing that God has granted and trusted you with. I wondered why he gave me four children but I am ever grateful that he trusted me with them and their upbringing. Yes, I made a lot of mistakes but all in all, I did many more things right. Experience and God taught me how to mature and do things better. I regret not having as much time with them because I was out working to provide for them. I am grateful for what we had and that God brought us through many challenges. It was my job to care for them and prepare them for adulthood. They are on loan to us because ultimately they belong to Him. God trusted us to do this and we must lean on Him to help us with all things.

I have been raising my children for 30-plus years since they were spread out over the years. Even though it was hard and at times I came close to losing my mind, it was all worth it. I am so grateful to have four children who call me "mom". I am honored to be their mother and that God gave them to me. They each have a calling in their lives and special characteristics that God gave to them. I tried very hard to raise them in the "way they should go" so that later they would not depart from it." Their relationship with the Lord as adults is between them and the Lord. Love them unconditionally, and even if you don't agree with everything they do, do not judge them. Of course, as their mom, you care about their lives. They are grown now and have to make their own choices and learn their lessons. I would love my children to learn from my mistakes, but usually, that does not happen. Many times they have to learn from their own mistakes. Continue to support them and leave their guidance and wisdom to God. It is hard, I know, but it will give you less worry and stress. Many times all you can do is pray for them, so be fervent and frequent in your prayers for them. If they do not listen to you much, pray that God puts someone in their paths that will comfort them and lead them in a Godly way.

One more thing I want to say to you. I know looking back as a single parent, there will be a lot of regrets. There will be times when it sounds as if you are making excuses for your shortcomings. Give yourself a break. As a parent, most of us do what we know and think is best at the time. At certain times, as we are raising our children, we only have a certain amount of knowledge. Do not beat yourself up about things that happened years ago. Your children may choose to blame you for things going on in their adult years. Some of it may be due to some mistakes you made as a parent. Sit down with them; hear them out when they are an adult, if they are struggling with anything from their childhood. Apologize to them and understand that this may not be enough. Some of your children as adults will want to continue to blame you.

At some point, after discussion and apologizing, it is up to them to be accountable for what is going wrong in their lives. They are adults and are making their own choices. If they are struggling with things from their childhood, they can get counseling and work through these things. If they are unwilling to do so, do not continue to take the "blame" for their poor adult decisions. At some point, you have to stop apologizing and feeling bad. It is not healthy for us to continue to beat ourselves up. We need to move on and leave it in the Lord's hands. This is not a copout. This is reality. As we age, we have to at some time focus on taking care of ourselves and letting our children do the same.

The best you can give to your children and grandchildren is your health and long life. If you continue to stress or help them out in things they should be doing for themselves, it will take a toll on you emotionally and physically. We all still have callings in our lives and we need to continue to walk in these. Our focus is to be a support system, to love unconditionally, and to care for ourselves (finally). Please take your health, both mental and physical, seriously.

Lastly, raising your children as a single parent is very difficult. Give yourself breaks often and don't be too hard on yourselves. Those who judge you have no idea how hard this is. Reach out to agencies and your church for help. Don't believe that you have to do this alone; you do not. The Lord is your strength along with all those others that He has put in your life. Do not be too proud to accept help. Remember to stay humble and flexible, for the Lord is in this with you. Praise Him daily and ask Him for your daily bread. He will provide for you and your children daily. Always have a grateful heart. He is always there with us even though we may not feel it. Pray for discernment and wisdom for guidance in everything and He will show you the way.

Pray over your children daily, along with teaching them that they can lean on God at all times. Model the behavior and beliefs that you want your children to have. Be positive and always reward good behavior. Resist giving so much attention to the negative because then you will get more negative behavior. Understand they are children and not adults, so allow them to make mistakes. This is how we all learn. Try to encourage them and guide them. A lesson I learned the hard way, we were made to be their parents, not to control them. We are to guide them and teach them for that is the job that our Lord gave to us.

He trusted us to raise them in His way and to learn age-appropriate lessons. Be careful what they listen to and what they hear, who their friends are, and how much space you allow them. As they become teenagers, draw closer to them and not give them more space. They need you to help make so many important decisions. Don't nag them or harass them, even though as teenagers they will believe that is all you do to them.

What an honor to be given these children. It is very difficult to raise children, especially in this world we live in. There are many resources to help you through this long, arduous path. Reach out for help and guidance. When you have done all you can do, stand strong and in prayer. God will reward you for doing the very best that you can. This is not about being perfect, so forgive yourself for your shortcomings and mistakes. Learn from them and be gentle to yourself. Submit all things to the Lord in prayer, and He will work them out. When you have finished your journey of raising your children, continue to be their mother (you are no longer their mom). At this time, if your relationship is healthy, you can now be their friend. Being their friend as they are growing up can be difficult. You are in a guiding and disciplining role, so leave friendship until they are an adult. I am so grateful that I have a personal relationship with my Lord and that He brought me through the time of raising my children. I had to learn as I went and I am thankful that I reached out and had His wisdom to guide me. It is never too late to learn or change, so be open for guidance and a better way. We continue to grow, learn, and change as we grow older. We never stop until it is time to go "home".

Count yourself blessed that you were given the honor of being a parent and that you have the resources out there to help you. Now that my children are grown, I get to sit back and be amazed at the awesome people they have become. Now, I can focus on grandchildren, and help my children raise their children. What an honor and a blessing to now be called a grandmother or "Mimi". It is a special love that I was never prepared for but I am so very grateful for. God bless you through your journeys and remember, He is always there to help us! Reach out constantly and He will guide and bless you, daily!

Chapter Eight
Sexual Addiction

At first, I was unsure whether I wanted to write about this issue that I encountered in my dating relationships. I am a Christian and many Christians are not comfortable with talking about sex. Since this is such a widespread issue and it affects so many people, I felt led to write about my experience and research into this topic to help the many men and women affected by this addiction.

When I wrote this chapter, about 10 years ago, statistics stated that in CHRISTIAN families alone, 49% of households have problems with porn. That is JUST the statistics in Christian families. Now, 68% of church-going men and over 50% of pastors view porn regularly! ("15 Mind-blowing Statistics About Pornography and the Church." Missionfrontiers.org 2020)

As you can imagine, the percentages in non-Christian families would be much higher. I am astounded at the high percentages, but then it is not exactly an addiction that is talked about openly. Sex addiction is like any other addiction and has similar characteristics to alcohol and drug addictions. In time, the addiction grows. With the growth, so does the preoccupation and frequency of sex and the use of porn. Eventually, the sex addict's partner is very hurt and confused, and usually, these relationships break up. Many times, the person that is involved in this addiction, goes outside their relationships to "get their fix".

One thing that I want to make clear is that this is not an addiction to sex or porn, it is an addiction to fantasy. Multiple sex partners or an increase in sex frequency along with the use of porn are just symptoms of this addiction. The use of porn is usually the foundation of this addiction. The fantasy is about forms of "perverse" sexual acts along with these acts being done with someone different. The majority of sex addicts are men, but a rising number of women are becoming addicted also. I will mainly focus on a male sex addict since this is what I have the most experience with. The symptoms, characteristics, behaviors, and consequences are the same regardless of gender.

This addiction is not unique to any race, financial, social, or marital status—Christian or non-Christian. It affects all men and women from all walks of life. Due to the availability of porn both in sex shops and on the internet, this addiction is growing. There are over 48 million Porn websites! (Above reference). What also needs to be considered is the "normalization" of perverse sexual practices. As we show more sexual material on TV and in movies, our morals continue to decline, and this addiction continues to grow and thrive. The key thing I want to stress also is that long after the issue has gotten worse and has become an addiction, the addict has no clue that it is "that bad".

Since this is an addiction to fantasy –there is little reality involved. Most of the time this addiction starts with the occasional use of porn. Most people believe that if you are not in a relationship, isn't it alright to watch porn to sexually satisfy yourself? As a Christian, it is never acceptable to watch porn or look at porn of any kind. We are taught, through God's Word, that we are to guard the window to our soul and spirit – our eyes, our mind, and our heart. The use of porn of any kind is allowing Satan to operate in us – this is not Godly behavior and will reap very un-Godly consequences.

In time, because we can become a "slave" to our bodily pleasures, we begin to watch/use it more and more. It all seems very innocent at the time. As we begin to fantasize more, we sometimes begin to go online and have different forms of sexual chat. This has become much easier over the years to do and now with webcams, more intimate and more "abnormal". We even start to think about swinging and getting involved in different sexual avenues outside of our committed relationships.

Many difficult things start to happen with the partner of an addict as time goes on – even before the issue advances to the addict level. At first, the woman starts to doubt herself. She does not understand why her man feels he needs "extracurricular activities" outside of their intimate times together. It starts to cause self-doubt in the woman, even the most beautiful and sexiest woman! It is very HARD to understand this addiction and many times the man himself does not understand what he is doing. After all, isn't it innocent watching or using porn once in a while?

The truth of the matter, and what I have experienced, this addiction is like cancer. It starts very "innocent" and the man feels that it is no big deal because all men do this, right? Then as the perversion gets embedded into his spirit and mind, he naturally wants more. Access to it is so easy, so it is no problem to use it more. Before the man knows it, the cancer has spread. Many times, it will destroy families, and marriages and cause the man to eventually lose their job. All this will happen before he realizes how serious the problem is and has become. Like any addict of any substance, something serious has to happen before the addict wakes up and realizes that there is truly an issue.

The addict gets so obsessed with the activity and feeding his habit – like drugs and alcohol that it takes over many areas of the addict's life. Once he realizes that he has a problem, many times it already has advanced. The addict can become depressed because he cannot realize that this "thing has him", not "he has it"! It soon becomes a huge consumer of time and energy, with the addict focusing on not much else.

They miss work due to depression or due to increased activity that takes over their normal schedule. Eventually, like any addict, they can lose their job. They further sink into depression because they cannot provide for their families with their lives spiraling so far out of control. Up to this point, they felt that they did not have an issue and certainly not one that could take over their life so fully.

While all this is happening to the addict, the woman partner has already gone through quite an emotional upheaval. She has gone through all of self-doubt and drop in confidence, due to not understanding what is happening. The man will tell her, it is not her and it is something that has to do only with him, but that does not help. No matter how many times I heard that, I still thought there was something wrong with me. I also felt that he was no longer attracted to me or wanted intimacy just with me, and that was very hurtful. It was damaging to our relationship, including creating doubt and mistrust in the relationship. It was natural to think that if he needed this 'extra' in his life, that sooner or later, he would need 'extra' that included another woman. Many times this does happen and there are many affairs outside of his committed relationship.

Another issue that comes up is that some men start asking their partners to engage in sexual activities they see on the screen or read about. If people can do that in the film or in the magazine, then why can't it be done in your relationship? The partner doesn't want to say no because they fear losing that partner to affairs where other women may perform these acts. It starts the partner questioning their values and norms. How far will the partner go for the addict to keep (in her mind) them "at home'. What the woman does not realize is the nature of this addiction, like any other, is that it will continue to grow. Even if the woman does everything the addict wants, eventually it will not be enough.

As stated earlier, with addictions, as time goes on, it takes more and more to satisfy them. What worked for them a few months ago, will no longer work. As time goes on, it is usually inevitable that there will be cheating involved. Let me say that this addiction, like others, is a sickness. I use the cancer analogy since it grew similarly. Without treatment, it will grow unchecked and will have dire consequences. We will discuss some of those a little later on. In my relationship, my partner eventually found someone online who was married and looking for attention from a man, any man.

The addict will either find someone with the same sickness at any level, to participate in online activities with them, or someone locally. They will also find those who will do anything to get attention from a man. It is very exciting for the addict to "be in charge" of someone else's sexual life. I am not trying to be crude here, but real. I am sharing my knowledge and experiences to help others. My ex-partner enjoyed telling the married woman (with whom he was having an affair), when, and how she was to have sex with him or her husband.

So, now he was an addict and he was attracting another person to porn and possibly leading them down the same path that he had come. Yes, I know that this woman is an adult and has choices to make. To get any kind of attention from a man, she was willing to do just about anything. This is sad but a reality in today's world. Again, like cancer, this sickness has passed to another due to both of these two people and their choices. Now there is another family involved. Earlier I would have said that if this woman had a relationship with God, she might have been less likely to look to a man for validation of any kind. Now that I know it is so prevalent in Christians also, I cannot always say that. It is sad what can happen when someone is attention-deprived. Also, to "invite" the enemy into your life it takes a "small crack in that door".

The internet is full of lonely people and very fertile ground for these types of liaisons. This relationship led to her coming to visit my ex-partner several times. In her emotional deficiency, she was becoming attracted to fantasy also. Not only to use porn but the fantasy of having adulterous affairs that would (in her mind) satisfy her need for attention. The sad part about this is that I don't feel that my ex-partner cared about her. Once she would hit town and "perform" their fantasies, he was ready for her to leave a day or so later. So, what she was looking for, she was not getting. Here is another woman affected by this addiction, and willing to do many immoral things to get attention from a man.

In my research about Sex Addiction, I learned that the addict wants love like all of us do. They will usually have a loving partner in their life, someone who is caring for them and standing by them. They become so obsessed with fantasy and all the characteristics of the addiction, that they end up losing that person. I know, at first, as I saw things progressing, I thought I could "help" my partner. After all, why would I not "stick by my man"? It took me a while, but I realized what most partners of sex addicts eventually realize – you cannot help them. This is truly something that they have to own, admit the issue they have, and seek their help for it.

There are many groups out there to help Sex Addicts. They have Sex Anonymous like they have Drug and Alcohol Anonymous. There are also Anon groups for the partners. I strongly recommend that even if your partner does not seek help for his addiction for a while, you can as the partner that is affected. I went to these meetings for a while and they helped me greatly. Some wives decide to stay with their husbands, and some decide to leave the marriage. It is an individual choice and it mainly is based on whether the addict gets help and sticks with it. You cannot help someone who does not want help. They have to acknowledge their addiction and seek help for it.

They will not do so until they are ready. Nothing the partner does or says will help this process along. I learned that the hard way. I didn't give up for a long time. My ex-partner eventually had to leave me and our relationship. After he cheated with the married woman, he committed to be faithful and to try again. I did not fully understand the nature of this addiction, so I stayed a few more years. Finally, as we were beginning to talk about taking the next step, he decided he wanted to end the relationship. I am fully convinced that he was fighting the temptation to contact that woman again and engage in cheating again. Rather than break his promise to me not to cheat on me again, he chose to leave our relationship. The temptation to continue with his fantasies was too great, and he eventually found someone "to leave me for".

The end of this relationship, which many would have said ended earlier, was devastating to me. I invested a lot of time and a lot of my heart into this relationship. It was a serious relationship, and we had been through so much together. Most importantly, I felt that I could be myself with him – he was my best male friend. There was a strong tie and bonds there that were hard to let go of. I knew he still was in love with me, but the addiction had changed everything. It had taken time to grow and I never knew that it would become such an addiction. This is the reason I am writing about this.

I cannot tell women what they should do if their partner is a Sex Addict. I can only tell you that you have to NOT doubt yourself. You also need to seek help for yourself. You must let your partner realize that they have an issue. If they are not willing to recognize their addiction or go for help, there is not much you can do to help them. You should focus on helping yourself. The key is to get emotionally healthy. There are anonymous groups along with Sex Addiction groups similar to drugs and alcohol. The anonymous groups help partners of the Sex Addict understand what is happening with the addict, how not to enable them, and the fact that there will be setbacks.

Sex addicts are looking for the same thing most of us are – LOVE! They want to love and be loved just like the rest of us. They can have a very wonderful partner and lose that partner because they cannot control their addiction. Being addicted to sex (fantasy) is very similar to being addicted to alcohol or drugs. The more you have, the more you want. There will become a time that it will rule your life and you will even find it hard to go to work. You can become depressed once you realize how far gone the addiction is and how much it has taken over your life. Pretty soon it is all you can think about and all you can be involved in.

Eventually, it will seriously affect the important relationships in your life. You will not be able to communicate very well, as you will be trying to hide what it is you are doing. Your life becomes two-sided; the normal and the "dark" side. As the "dark" side grows, it encroaches on the normal. An addict will try to hold onto the normal side for as long as they can, convincing themselves that the "dark" side is contained and under control! As the "dark" side grows (like a cancer) it will eat away at the normal part of your life. It will become the main part of your life long before you realize it. You will convince yourself that you have things under control LONG after you don't!

Usually, like a drug or alcohol addiction, something major has to happen in the addict's life before they will realize what truly is going on. An important relationship will end, the addict may lose their job, family members or co-workers will find out, or the addict will have done something illegal. The "rock bottom" for the addict usually has to happen before they realize that there is a huge problem and they need help

If you are a Christian and have had sexual fantasies about someone else other than your partner, it is called adultery. (Matthew 5:27-28) KJV. You have looked at another and lusted after them in your heart, it is the same as committing that sin. You have turned something beautiful (sex), into something ugly, selfish, and damaging. If you are married, then you have been unfaithful to your spouse. If single, you are sinning against the dear person you may one day marry. If you are returning to this behavior over and over again, despite your desire to stop, then you are out of control.

If you are saved, the first step is to admit there is a problem. The second is to bring this sin under the authority of God. It is called a "stronghold" and Satan uses this to keep you bound up and unable to follow God. You are involved in a spiritual battle and it cannot be battled in the flesh. Our flesh is weak and we constantly have to ask for God's help to battle our temptations. Do not doubt your salvation but instead confess your sin and ask God to forgive it. Then begin the process of getting help. As stated earlier, there are Sex Anonymous groups that you can attend. Along with those groups, seek out solid Christian counseling. Most of all, daily ask God to help you with this addiction. Give the whole thing to Him and constantly seek His assistance. When you give it to Him 100% and are constantly seeking his help, you will be able to overcome this stronghold.

Remember, that similar to a drug and alcohol addict, once you are healed, you will still have to be careful. Continuous prayer and laying of your life before God will help you stay "clean." There are many groups out there for Christian men and women who will support you and help you maintain an addiction-free life. Research and use all of the support that is out there along with God so that you may live a life free of any addiction. You will be much happier. As part of your healing, God may use you to testify to other men and women, so that they may know that they are not alone and it is very possible to heal from this issue.

Prayer is the most effective method for overcoming any sin in your life. Here's how to pray, every day…

1. Confess all known sin
   Psalm 51 | Mark 7:20-23 | 1 John 1:7-10
2. Renounce conformity to the world
   Romans 12:2, 6:13-14
3. Ardently seek an intimate relationship with Jesus Christ. He will give you a richer, more meaningful life.
   John 10:10, 15:5-12 | Ephesians 3:14-19 | Philippians 3:10-14

4. Offer your body as a "living sacrifice" to God
   Romans 12:1-2 | 1 Corinthians 6:19-20
5. Worship God
   John 4:23-24 | Philippians 3:3
6. Thank and praise God. Thank Him for his grace and mercy, praise Him, and keep seeking His mercy. Thank God for the answered prayer.
   What should we thank God for, and how should we praise Him? | Thanksgiving, do the right thing | Are you thankful to God? | Philippians 4:6-7 | Colossians 4:2
7. Ask God for help in living a pure and loving life
   Philippians 4:6-7 | Hebrews 4:16

(Save Yourself Some Pain; 7 Tips for New and Growing Christians, Christananswers.net)

Another way to combat sin in your life is to read and memorize scriptures. We need to "hide the Word" in our hearts so that it will be there to draw on in our difficult times. We need to spend regular time in God's Word, meditating on it daily. When we memorize scriptures, we will be able to bring them to mind in our prayers and whenever we need them. A regular time each day spent with the Lord, will help us walk in His will and not in ours. We have a natural sinful nature and without a personal relationship with the Lord and regular time spent in His Word with Him, we will find it easier to fall into sin.

Chapter Nine
The Consequences and Behaviors of Abuse

When you are abused as a child, there is not a lot you can do about it, except tell someone. There are a lot of emotions that will flood your heart when this is happening to you. Mainly you will learn survival techniques to "manage" the abuse. You will also be taught that there might be something wrong with you or you are misbehaving. No one punishes a child unless they deserve it – right? Since there is not a lot you can do to control the situation, you may think the answer is to run away. That does not always work either, as described in my teenage year's chapter.

The main thing that you can do is to tell someone. A trusted teacher, confidante, principal – anyone who will listen. You want to be sure you tell someone that you can trust, and they only tell those who can help you, not everyone. There is a lot of shame in admitting to an adult that your family has this horrific problem and that you are living in this awful environment. Back in those days, probably not a lot would have been done about it. Today, it is different, and the path to take.

If you are being abused as an adult, there is a lot that you can do. Many people, who have not been in an abusive relationship, cannot understand why women stay when this is happening to them. There are many reasons that this happens, one being that they have been through this as a child. When you grow up abused as a child, you become "used" to this environment. You are programmed to believe that you must have done something wrong, and that is why you are being "punished". Also, growing up as an abused child you feel that you were not loved, and possibly are unlovable. Your self-esteem is in the negative column.

So, when as an adult, you find yourself in an abusive relationship, it is hard to know what to do at first. Since you may have grown up like this, when the first violence happens, you are not as shocked. It is something that you are familiar with, and have become accustomed to. The first question that goes through your mind is "What did I do wrong now"? You spend a lot of time analyzing your actions and what you may have done to "deserve" this abuse.

When you are being abused (like as a child), you are being hit and not defending yourself. So as this goes on, you train yourself not to protect yourself. Then you believe that you are not worthy of love or protection. Many times as an early adult, when I tried to get help or protection, they never did anything to protect me. That showed me that it was possible that I did not deserve protection. No one would step up and protect me. Many times I was made to be the bad person and I was wrong because I sought help from the authorities. I was asked one time by someone in authority, "What did I do to deserve the beating"?

Due to the abuse coming from a loved one, there is a battle that ensues within us. We want to flee the abuse to a safe environment, but that means leaving a loved one in a family environment. This environment, under normal circumstances, is supposed to protect and care for us; just as our loved ones are supposed to do. So we are in conflict as we try to protect ourselves which may mean leaving a loved one and our family.

Trying to fight this battle within us along with trying to figure out the logistics of escape sometimes is more energy than we may possess. It is very difficult to leave and takes a lot out of us. Many people outside of the situation cannot understand why we stay. They don't understand that we may have been brainwashed through emotional and mental abuse by the same person who physically abuses us.

Physical abuse is more dynamic and easier to prove if bruises or broken bones are present. Emotional and mental abuse is harder to prove and harder to stop. It can be overt and it can be much more subconscious.

Our partner convinces us that we are not worthy of love, protection or to be cared for. When the abuse occurs, we think that we do deserve this. The truth is we do deserve to be treated with respect, consideration, and kindness, and we are worthy of protection and healthy love.

The longer we stay with someone who abuses us, in any way, the more we learn to make excuses for them. We cannot wrap our minds around the possibility that someone who claims to love us could also hurt us so deeply. We can see it much easier if it was happening to a sister, best friend, or a child of ours. We would not tolerate it and would want to do something severe to make it stop.

With us, this does not happen in the same way. Not only do we make excuses and feel we are to blame, we have trouble seeing what is happening in a realistic light. We are so damaged emotionally and mentally, that we can no longer see clearly. We thereby have a distorted view of what is happening and what we are truly feeling.

When it happens to one of our kids or friends, there is usually someone else to protect them. We have no one because the person who was supposed to protect us is abusing us. We don't even have ourselves, much of the time. We are so "beaten" down by the abuse and not knowing what is going on, that we cannot think clearly. We are scared to leave, especially if that person has used physical abuse on us. We fear that if we leave, it will get worse. We fear that this person will find us and hurt us further, even to the extent of killing us. Many times they threaten us with statements telling us that they will kill us if we even think about leaving.

The thing that we need to think long and hard about, as women, is that the first time we are hit we are a victim. After repeated abuse, we become volunteers for the abuse. In not doing anything to stop the abuse or to leave the abuse, we are teaching our abusers that it is acceptable for them to continue to do this. Leaving is a choice, as is deciding to stay.

When I finally saw that my partner was not serious about getting help so that we may save the marriage, I had to make a decision. At that time, I did not feel strong enough in my esteem and was not totally in a place where I wanted to protect myself. I was mixed up with feelings about not wanting to give up on the marriage. I believed in marriage and in trying to stay married, as divorce wasn't an option that I wanted to explore. I know in the Bible that God is against divorce.

The Bible does discuss when there are incidences of adultery, that God does accept divorce. I had to do some soul-searching and digging into the Word, to finally accept that God would not want me to stay in a marriage where I was in danger along with our son. Adultery did in the end, enter into the picture, so the reason I left was for both of these reasons. The main reason I left was for the abuse.

Sadly, since I was not feeling great about myself and my self-worth, in the end, the driving factor for me taking the large step of leaving was my 1.5-year-old son. My instincts to protect myself were almost non-existent, but my maternal instinct to protect my son was intact. I remember just before I realized that it was time, my ex-husband would call out my name in a certain tone that would upset my young son. He instinctively knew that something bad was about to follow. He had learned through being in our household to fear and to know when something bad was about to happen.

I finally woke up at least to the fact that I was teaching something to my child that I never wanted any child to ever have to learn. When I was finally able to leave my childhood home, at the age of 18, I vowed that I would never allow another child to be abused or witness abuse! What was I allowing my son to learn, see, and live in? It was so against what I wanted for him. If I could not leave for me to protect myself, I must leave for him and to protect him. It was my duty as his mother, to keep him from all things evil, threatening and that would hurt him in any way.

Many abusers are men, who control the money in the household. Believe me, I know that leaving is not easy. Abusers isolate the victim from family and friends as a matter of control. They control most of what the victim does so it is very hard for the victim to figure out logistically how to leave. As the abuser loses control and the victim changes or talks about leaving, things get escalated. It is very scary and can be extremely dangerous.

In our society now, there are places where a victim and the children can go that will protect them and give them safety. There are hotlines where you can call to get help along with shelters. Along with these things that can be used to help, planning can also be extremely helpful. If there is any way to put aside some money, do so. If the abuser is in complete control, then at least figure out how to get some of your things out of the house. Maybe take a little at a time to a friend's or family member's house for later. You can leave and run to a family member's home, but remember that is the first place that the abuser will look.

As much as possible, it is imperative to plan. Make a plan and set goals, without changing your routine. When it gets time to go, go to a shelter where you and your children will be protected and the abuser cannot find you. The shelter will help you and give you guidance on what to do next.

I want to address one thing that I also think is very important. I did call the police on numerous occasions but did not press charges. That was counterproductive. I thought that if I called the police, I would scare him into behaving correctly and not hitting me. With repeated calls, it did not accomplish that. Nowadays, I believe if a victim calls the police and there is evidence of abuse, the police will take him in regardless of whether you press charges or not. They have finally decided this because victims are afraid to press charges and they want to protect the victim. If you are in danger, you need to call the police. Be ready for them to do their job, and do not interfere when they take the abuser in custody.

Most abusers will not get better unless they get help. I learned the hard way, that the abuser does not usually pre-mediate that they are going to hurt you. Many times, they get angry and lose control. We all get angry, but most of us do not cross the line to do physical damage to a person or other objects. People who abuse do need help and that help needs to be professional. This behavior can be corrected over time with the right kind of help.

Without this help, this abuser will continue to abuse. Whether it is one person, or other people after a victim leaves. Most are serial abusers and will remain so if they do not get help. There are also serial victims. Unless the victim gets professional help, they may leave one abuser, only to go to another one. They learn how to "survive" in this type of environment, where it can become a "known" and a "comfortable" existence. Unless they receive professional help, this is all they will ever know. It takes work to become mentally and emotionally healthy.

When we stay in these abusive relationships, we make many excuses for our partners. We say that they are doing these things now, but when this or that happens, they will be doing better. When you marry a man, you should not marry a man based on his "potential", because that is not what is happening now. You cannot predict the future. Similarly, do not let the abuser make excuses or do not make excuses for them. We all have choices and should understand that we truly have to live in the here and now.

The violence cycle is a hard one. Another reason the victim doesn't leave, is they are remembering the kind, sweet, caring person that the abuser used to be or is between the violent incidents. I remember after the violence, my ex-husband would become very sorry, romantic, sweet, and kind. He would say he was sorry, and many times would buy me flowers. He would even want to have sex afterward. I think that he felt if I allowed him to do so, then everything would be ok between us thereby I would be over the incident.

The problem with that is, if you are not alright with that after the violence, would you say so? You would be afraid that if you didn't let him have sex with you, he would get violent again. That is having sex under duress and many times it can even be rape. When you are afraid that if you say no, you will get beaten again, so you relent, that is not consensual sex. Just because the person is your partner, it does not give them the right to have sex without your desire and total consent to do so.

Once a victim is safely out of an abusive situation, they must get counseling. We need to figure out what is wrong with our thinking. Why do we possibly attract someone who is like this? What beliefs do we have about ourselves? What is emotional health and what does an emotionally healthy relationship look like? It will take time to heal from the abuse and to work on you. Just as it took time to get damaged, it will take time to recover. It will also be a work in progress to become emotionally healthy.

As you are healing, and growing, be sure to be thankful for the process you are making. Give yourself plenty of time. Also, while this process is going on, be sure to work on forgiving the abuser. Forgiveness is important in your recovery. It is important for you, not for the person who hurt you. I have written a separate chapter about forgiveness since it is so vital to our growth and healing.

I will close this chapter with some warning signals that MAY mean that a person could be an abuser. If even a few of these signals are present along with your intuition, you should be concerned.

1. In the beginning of the relationship, things move at a fast pace. They are looking for a commitment, living together, and marriage prematurely.
2. They are verbally abusive.
3. They resolved conflict with intimidation, bullying or violence.
4. They break things or strike things when angry.
5. They have abused others in prior relationships
6. They use excuses for their abuse such as drugs or alcohol
7. They have had encounters with the police for violent behaviors.
8. They refuse to accept rejection
9. They are controlling and very jealous
10. They enlist the help of friends and or family of their partner to help them keep a relationship.
11. They show signs of or stalk their partners.
12. They often suffer mood swings or are angry or depressed.
13. They consistently blame others for what is wrong in their life.
14. They have weapons and feel the weapons are a part of their persona.
15. They have seen or experienced violence in their childhood.

While having one or two of the signals does not mean that they will be or are abusers, they are things to be aware of. Your intuition will be the key to clearly assessing whether someone could be an abuser. Many times we ignore our intuition and our "inner voices". We must be very open and honest with ourselves while listening to our "gut." This will allow us to prevent many of the events or bad treatment in our lives. While you can't prevent every bad thing, there are many that we can.

Last, I want to ask that once you are safe, out of the abusive situation, healed, and back on your feet, please help someone else. There are so many others out there going through what we have survived. I feel it is only right to help others get out of the abuse. No one will understand totally what we have gone through, except someone who has also gone through it. As you know, when we are in this abuse, we don't listen to many people. The only one we may listen to would be someone who truly knows what we are going through and they have lived it. I feel that we must help others. I have lived this throughout my life and writing this book is just one way I am accomplishing this. I think it is so important for us to be a vital part of the solution once we have lived it and survived it!

Chapter Ten

My Military Life

I joined the military at the age of 18. Even then my enlistment papers needed to be signed by both parents. As you can tell by earlier chapters, my home life and childhood were full of abuse from my mother. I wanted to go to college after I graduated from High School. I had saved some money from working jobs from the ages 16-18. I thought I could go to the local school because that was in my budget. That would mean living at home. It became more apparent from at least the age of 16 years old that I could not continue to do that.

I strongly felt a need for peace of mind and physical safety. So that as soon as I graduated from High School, I would have to leave. During the spring semester of my senior year, I began talking to an Army Recruiter. At that time in 1973, we were starting to pull out of the Vietnam War. They were talking about disbanding the draft in the next few years. Women were not allowed to be in combat, but because they knew that in a few years, the enlistment numbers were going to drop due to no draft, they opened more non-combat jobs to women.

At this time, the WAC (Women's Army Corp) was in effect. Women who came into the Army were a separate entity from the men. The headquarters for the WAC was in Mobile, Alabama. That is where I ended up doing Basic Training. I was interested in Personnel Management. I joined on October 30, 1973. I knew that I needed to leave my home and the Army promised me a duty station in California. I was also very interested in the military paying my College expenses through the GI Bill program.

I went to Basic Training for 8 weeks at Ft McClellan. I then came home for Christmas break. After that, I went to Ft Ord, California to do my typing school. I then traveled to Ft Benjamin Harrison, Indianapolis, Indiana. Here I did Personnel Management Specialist School. It was here that I met my ex-husband, another service member. This is discussed in a previous chapter.

Next was my first permanent duty station - back at Ft Ord, California. Since I had gotten married about 6-8 months after arriving, I applied for and received a compassionate reassignment to Ft Shafter, Honolulu, Hawaii. I stayed there 2 years and then became interested in changing my job in the military to a Lab Technician (hospital). I moved to Ft Sam Houston, San Antonio, Texas. It was quite a culture shock from Hawaii.

Once I finished my Lab Technician School, I was stationed there at Ft Sam Houston. I spent 3 years there, having my firstborn in Oct 1977 and going through a divorce. I finished almost 6 years of active duty by this time.

To feel safe, I moved to Colorado and moved directly into the Army Reserve from Active Duty. I started my life in Colorado in 1979. I would go on to do about 17 more years on Active Reserves and spend a few years in the inactive Reserves. I was moved to inactive Reserves during my 19th year of total service time. I was told to do correspondence courses to make sure I earned enough points to get my 20 years and retire at the age of 60. The reason I had to be moved to inactive from active Reserves was due to weight. They were very strict at that time and I was having trouble losing my "baby weight" from my 4th child.

In 2015, as I was a few months from turning 60, I contacted the Records Department to see how I could apply for the retirement that was due me at the age of 60. It was at that time that I was informed that their records stated that I only had 18.2 "good" years of points and I would not be getting a retirement. You can imagine I was pretty upset. They said the only way to fight that was to produce my Leave and Earning Statements for all my time in service. I did not have those, and it would be very difficult to get them.

I went through the process to find medical records from active duty many years ago and they could not be found. Some things medically could be found in those records and since they were lost, it was going to be difficult.

Now would be a good time to discuss some things that happened to me in the military that would not be in my medical records. In my early times in Hawaii, while on active duty, I endured many instances of sexual harassment. Both comments and inappropriate touching from my First Sergeant and several doctors in the ER during exams. They made me extremely uncomfortable and this was happening quite a bit to female soldiers.

When in the late 1970s, the Women's Divisions of each branch of service were brought together with the Men's division, there was no discussion about how to act around each other. I guess the leadership thought it would be knowledge that everyone would already possess. Unfortunately, the thinking of many male soldiers was that a female in the military was a tramp and looking for "hook-ups." To this day I don't know if they believed that or if that was their excuse for being inappropriate to the women.

As mentioned before in the chapter about my ex-husband, at the same time that the sexual abuse was happening, I was dealing with abuse from him. During that era, women who were being sexually abused did not tell anyone. If you did it would continue to make you a victim over and over. Many of us kept it to ourselves. I would go on sick calls a lot to get out of the office, and away from my First Sergeant. With the abuse that was happening during several ER visits for asthma, I started asking for a female doctor. If I had to be seen by a male doctor, I would ask for a female chaperone.

The one thing that never ran through my mind was that any of this sexual abuse was my fault. Unlike child abuse and marital abuse, I knew that it was inappropriate and not warranted by any actions from me. It is sad to me that this was "accepted" behavior at that time. If you did try to tell anyone, no one would listen. The only way I knew how to deal with it at the time was to "stuff" it and try to now think about it. I was dealing daily with abuse in my home and that was already too much to deal with.

All these instances that happened were discussed with no one. My best friend of almost 60 years was shocked to hear about all of this in the past few years. Once I turned 60, work and caring for others slowed down, these things started to surface. I knew that there were things that were weird about my behavior at doctor's offices, not sitting with my back to the door of a restaurant, and the many short fuses I had in dealing with life happenings. I thought my lack of patience was due to the stress in my life. I also am very claustrophobic and cannot handle crowds.

Four years ago, I went to see a psychiatrist and was diagnosed with PTSD. Things started to make sense to me about where all of my issues stemmed from. I started a long battle to receive some compensation from the military for this PTSD, especially from Military Sexual Trauma. As I said earlier, I didn't tell anyone about these incidents, so there were no records of any of them. This made it hard for anyone to believe me.

Throughout my life, there seemed to be a common thread of misbelief and no one protecting me. Many times the police were called for spousal abuse. When I finally did press charges, they were dropped. When I told others about the abuse as a child, I was not believed. When I finally told of my spousal abuse, I was not believed. When I filed for compensation for PTSD, many did not believe me. I filed two appeals and finally, after 4 years, I won some compensation. I finally told the right person, who also asked me the right questions and she believed me.

I have been in and out of counseling for years working hard to get through all the various abuses. My most recent counseling has been for Military Sexual Trauma since it just surfaced a few years ago. Counseling is a great avenue to work through abuse and to get emotionally and mentally healthy. It is not easy. You have two choices - use this trauma as a crutch for the rest of your life OR do the work and get through it. It is up to us to get through what life deals us and to be the best person we can be.

In 2019, I was asked to write a chapter in a book called "Resilient Women". It was an anthology that was 22 chapters long. there are 22 people/day that commit suicide due to PTSD. I was honored to write that chapter and in there I did discuss some of the above things that happened. I discussed some of the challenges that I had survived and I wanted to help others. Other women need to know that they can talk about it now and get the help they need. These things happened to many of us, so they can stop feeling so isolated and get the help they need.

Regardless of these challenges, I can say that my time in the military was a positive thing overall for me! It taught me a lot about teamwork, common goals, focus and I grew as a person. I learned a lot about others and myself. I learned I was much more capable than I had previously believed. Now as I am older, and my kids are grown up, having the VA as my insurance helps me tremendously. It is challenging at times, but at least I do have health care when I cannot afford premiums. It was also great to get my Bachelor's degree paid for with the GI Bill. I was able to travel, along with living in Hawaii. I met people from all over the United States and it broadened my horizons. I appreciate the benefits when they are available to us. It was meant for me to be in the military and even though there was quite a bit of various traumas, it added to my valuable lessons in life.

Chapter Eleven
Sexual Trauma and PTSD

I want to write about the rate of sexual trauma in our society today. It does not only happen with women; frequently it happens to boys also. We all know someone who experienced sexual trauma when they were young. Many times it is from a family member. If this has ever happened to you, I am praying you sought help. The help I am talking about is counseling. Many of us have not told anyone what has happened, but at some time, you need to do the work in counseling. Sexual trauma leaves many scars behind. Even if you "stuff" it for many years, the consequences will show up in all parts of your life.

One of the most obvious consequences is Post Traumatic Stress Disorder(PTSD). Trauma will leave you feeling like you are not worthy. It will also leave anxiety and very short patience spans. It will not take much of an incident to make you get upset. One everyday example is road rage. I have experienced this for years. I would not do anything to hurt anyone else, but my temper has a short string on it. You also will not be very patient with people or life. Many things can quickly make you angry. This is one of the reasons for therapy.

Another consequence of trauma is a lack of trust. If you have been sexually traumatized, you will have a very hard time trusting a person of the opposite sex. You may have trouble with "normal" sexual relations due to your trauma, also. It takes a lot of work to get through these things, but on the other side of that work, lies a true reward. There are truly enough problems in relationships today. Being emotionally healthy, having trust, and feeling free of the consequences of trauma is a big reward. Being able to have healthy relationships will make your life so much better.

Other consequences of trauma can be anxiety in crowds, in stressful situations, and trouble sleeping. All of these can have a huge impact on your health. Not sleeping well and being stressed a lot will give you blood pressure, and other diseases along with weight issues. Many of us tend to eat emotionally, so weight gain and being overweight is a serious health concern.

Suicide is a huge consequence of trauma. Many people give up because they can't see a way out of the pain in their life. Many people that have suffered trauma, do not get the help they need. For many reasons, they decline therapy. Some want it and cannot get it. Our Veterans, after coming home from war, are very mentally damaged. They have seen and had to do things in the military that are against what we believe to be right morally. This takes a huge toll on their psyche. In the Vietnam War for example, when the soldiers returned, they were told to not talk about anything they saw or did. Many did not go to therapy and had to deal with "personal hells" in their lives. Many had night terrors for many years. Many have PTSD that they have never gotten treatment for. The government through the VA system has been a long time in getting the therapy for them that they need. I have several members in my family who have struggled with this.

Now is a good time to discuss my sexual trauma and PTSD. I had many incidents in the late 1970s, within the first few years of my Military career. When I was stationed in Hawaii, I had extreme sexual harassment from one of my superiors. Inappropriate touching, actions, and comments went on for about two years. I also had inappropriate touching from several doctors when in the ER for asthma attacks. At the same time I was enduring this, I was married to another service member who was abusing me (see chapter on Abusive Marriage). Due to all these abuses happening at the same time, I "stuffed" the military ones for about 40 years. I forgot about them happening and of course did not tell anyone, not even my closest friend of many years. I chose to try and deal with the abuse I had in front of me daily instead. After almost 5 years of trauma, including sexual trauma, my marriage ended. It was very traumatic and scary.

For many years after, I was exhibiting symptoms of PTSD and did not know it. It wouldn't be until I was in my 60s, that I would be formally diagnosed and get treatment for this PTSD. My coping mechanisms have grown over the years, especially with raising four children, mostly on my own. When I was first diagnosed, I could see those symptoms all through my life. I just didn't know what they were. My lack of patience I thought was due to just the stress of life in general and, especially of being a single mom of 30+ years. I had very little trust in men and many problems in my relationships. One major problem was that I attracted the wrong men, mainly due to my not being emotionally healthy.

As we are writing this chapter and finishing up this book in 2024, I have been divorced for 44 years. I never remarried because as I was getting healthier emotionally, I never found someone worth making that commitment to. Someone that I could trust to be my partner in crime and to be around my children/grandchildren. I did have 2 long-term relationships during these 44 years, one lasting over 11 years. That relationship was very close to the friendship, "partner-in-crime" that almost led to marriage. That person developed an addiction that would later destroy our relationship.

Since that relationship ended about 17 years ago, I have decided to not date. If I meet someone who I think is a good marriage partner, I will court him to find out if it will work. I find that with the great female friends that I have and my relationship with the Lord, I am "not looking" for male companionship. A big part of that is also the friends who I have in my church that are men. It has taken many years to find a male friend who doesn't want something else from me. Maybe as I have gotten more emotionally and mentally healthy, this has been a nice side benefit. After all these years of being alone and learning how to love myself, I am content. Do I want to ever get remarried? Yes, but it will take someone honest, transparent, emotionally stable, and kind. I also would not only like a life partner, but a spiritual partner in ministry.

Back to talking about PTSD and sexual trauma. I experienced some of my trauma during my early years in the military. When I came in 1973, the women were in a separate service. Soon after coming in, the men and women were mixed with very little discussion about how men should treat women. Maybe the powers that be felt that were taught at home before joining the military? I cannot count the number of times I was told as a female soldier that I must have come into the military because I was a tramp and liked to have sex with many men. I believe that is their excuse for treating so many women poorly. Today, it is much better in the military but it still is a problem. Unfortunately, many female soldiers have horror stories to tell and consequently have developed PTSD. Women need to know what happened is not their fault. It is also very important to get therapy for their healing.

Again, at least 22 people per day commit suicide that are Veterans. I know of quite a few who have chosen that way out of their pain. Many wonderful nonprofits are out there to help. If you are depressed and feel like you are considering that option, please ask for help. I know it feels overwhelming, but the help is there. Many soldiers turn to drugs and alcohol, to numb the pain. This is a typical response to this deep pain. The problem with that is that the pain does not go away, it is just delayed. Also, alcohol is a depressant, so it has the opposite long-term effect.

It may take a long time to do the work to get to a point where you feel you have worked through your trauma. You will still have "triggers" but will be able to handle them better. If at any point you need more help, please do not hesitate to get it! Not all of your family and friends will understand what you have gone through. As long as they can be by your side as you work through it, that is great. One person who will "get it" is God. He has seen and known you before you were born. He has given you strengths that you may not know you have inside of you. He knew what you would go through. He is always right by your side; "He never leaves us nor forsakes us"! Lean on him to walk through life's challenges and ask Him to change your heart. You will need His help to forgive others so that you may feel free! This forgiveness is not for the other person but to free you! Unforgiveness and bitterness will eat you from the inside, outward. It can also cause many health issues.

Chapter Twelve
Breaking Up Is Hard To Do

I have discussed in an earlier chapter our behaviors and consequences of being in abusive relationships. I will discuss information/suggestions regarding leaving an abusive relationship. These pertain also to leaving any relationship that is not healthy.

Let me first say that I am not an advocate for divorce. The Bible tells us that God does not like divorce except in cases when adultery occurs. This does not mean that any time this happens this is a free "get out of the relationship" card. I struggled with my divorce greatly, even after 5 years of severe abuse. I was in a concentrated bible study at that time and was searching for God's Word on this subject. I believe two things are needed for a person to be healed of this stronghold of being an abuser. One is extensive counseling and the second is the removal of this root from their spirit by God.

The first thing a couple should do if there is any trouble in their relationship is to seek counseling. It is preferable that this counseling be faith-based due to usually it is a flesh nature at battle in the relationship. When you commit to someone, you are not only committed to them but more importantly, to the relationship. In today's world, people entering marriage sometimes think that if they get tired of someone, they can just leave. I suggest never using the divorce word or thinking about that option unless there is abuse or adultery. If it is never an option for relationships other than those two circumstances, then a couple will focus more on solving the issues in their relationship than leaving. Once someone uses the word "divorce" it changes the whole relationship. Couples that have been together for decades will tell you that they have lasted so long because they worked on it together and giving up was not an option.

The first option should always be counseling. If there is abuse present, and counseling does not work or the abuser refuses to go, then you may not have a choice but to separate, for your safety. A concerted effort must be made, especially if there are children involved. If there are safety issues, separation may be needed so that you can work on the relationship while remaining safe. Even in cases of adultery, it is not wise to automatically leave the relationship. Pray about it and see where the Lord leads you. It is very possible that if this is a situation that has happened only once and your partner is remorseful and wants to work on the relationship it would be worth saving. If there is a pattern, separation will be wise to decide whether divorce is the next step.

Again, as discussed in an earlier chapter, it is important to let someone you trust know what is happening. Many times abuse is hard to prove unless there are physical or mental signs. If the abuse is life-threatening, you should remove yourself as soon as possible. Many times, it is control, mind games, and can build starting as small things. At this time, it is wise to start documentation and sharing with a trusted friend or family member. The worst thing to do is to stay silent. It is typical behavior of an abuser to isolate you from your loved ones. This is a form of control. The more they can keep you isolated the more they can control you. In addition, no one will witness the abuse and therefore when you start to talk about it, you may have trouble with people believing you. I had this trouble with my ex-husband, due to him sometimes being a different person outside the home than he was with me at home.

Documenting what is happening is important because when these things happen it is hard to remember the details. You will see how often it is happening plus you will have information that you can share with someone else. First, it is important to share with one trusted friend that is your friend alone, and not a friend of both of yours. Next, you need to research your community where the shelters are. Even if you feel that you will never have to run to a shelter when you leave, they are a wealth of information for you. There are free counselors available, legal help, and other agencies that they can connect you with for help. If you do not have your own money, they can also help you if you need to leave immediately.

Speak with a counselor as soon as possible. If your partner is not willing to go with you to work on the relationship, you must do this for yourself. Not only will it help you begin to sort things out and see what is "normal" and what is "not normal", but it begins a process of documentation. This is very necessary if you end up needing to call the police to protect yourself, get a restraining order when necessary, or possibly file for a divorce. Documentation and having a plan, if your situation is dangerous, is imperative. There are many organizations out there to help you. If there are children in this relationship, through my experience with Child Protective Services, I would be wary of reporting anything to them at first. If you are instructed to through your counseling, then make sure you tap into all resources first. I am sad to say that through the experiences of many other persons close to me, they have not been treated properly or honestly by CPS, so be careful. You do not want to have additional issues along with what you are already dealing with. Of course, if a child's life is ever in danger, contact the police and they will contact CPS. Take steps wisely and with discernment, with much prayer and counseling.

Documenting, counseling, and becoming aware of all the agencies in your community that can help you are important first steps. They are part of the "plan" that is necessary to leave an abusive relationship. If you do not have your own money, some family members who can protect and provide for you, are very important. Many times, we stay in abusive relationships way too long. Whether we have become accustomed to the abuse, believe their lies that it won't happen again, or are just afraid to be alone or a single parent, we all stay longer than we should. On the flip side, in relationships other than abusive, it may take longer to leave. You feel as if you want to "try everything possible before giving up on a marriage. You don't want to have regrets later and think maybe you didn't try everything or give it enough time. You will know when you have done all you can. Throughout this process, always pray and work on yourself.

If you feel alone, feel that no one will believe you; please know that you are never alone. God is always there for you and will help you. Pray for wisdom, discernment, and strength whenever you need it. If you have been isolated because your partner is controlling or abusive, there are always agencies in your community that will help. I know that if you are being provided for by this person, it can be very difficult to understand how you can get out of this situation. Again, there is a lot of help out there for you. It is up to you to reach out to research and connect with these agencies. It will seem very overwhelming, especially if you are already dealing with so much. Remember that to change things for the better, you have to reach out. It will become easier as you find the support and help that you will need. It will give you hope and the ability to see a "light at the end of this dark tunnel".

When you are going through abuse and know that you might have to leave the relationship if counseling does not change things, please do not turn to another relationship. This will just make things even more difficult. It is tempting to believe someone that "they will protect" you but you will end up getting into more difficulties. It is never smart to engage in another romantic relationship to "run away" from your current issues or to "get even". If your partner committed adultery or is remorseful, try to work it out through counseling. If you get separated during this time to work on the relationship or to go through a divorce, it is not wise to engage in a new relationship during this time. It takes away the focus on your current relationship and can be used against you easily. If you go to another, can you be serious about working things through? It is always better, that if through all the counseling and working on the relationship, it does not work, to get divorced (for the reasons of abuse and adultery), before engaging in a new relationship. Not only does it not make the "waters muddy", it allows a proper grieving period before starting something else. It assures that a whole lot of unnecessary baggage will not go into a new relationship. Many times people get involved with another relationship before getting divorced or soon after the divorce. I will elaborate more on this later.

If after counseling, and trying very hard to work through the adultery or abuse, it still may not work and time to get a divorce. It is very painful, even if the main portion of the cause is your partner. Remember, there is never one side to an issue, there are always two. Even in abuse and control, we are responsible for how we react, and how we document or go for help. Not getting help, just allows it to continue. Without help, it never gets better. It is rare that it only happens once unless you leave after the first time, which most of us do not do.

If you have chosen to leave, and the situation is abusive, get a restraining order to protect yourself. Also, sometimes this does not work especially if you are dealing with an irrational person. If this is the case, you must go somewhere where you will be safe. It may have to be a shelter or a loved one that can protect you. Be very aware of your surroundings as you live your daily life and never be alone. Many times leaving, even for your safety, will not make your partner happy. Especially in situations where your partner is controlling. They will be upset that they have lost control of you and the relationship. Be careful, it can get dicey. That is why it is wise to have a plan, have documentation, and have counseling. The resources are out there for you. Please don't think that if you don't have money, you cannot get help. This is not true. Do your research, and have others outside of the situation help you throughout this long process. Again, be careful who you have helping you. Just let a select few into the situation and definitely whom you can trust implicitly.

I am well aware, as mentioned before, that we all stay in abusive, controlling, adulterous relationships for too long. We make excuses for ourselves, our partners, and our situation. We always think that it will get better, by itself or believe when our partner tells us so. With violence, there is a well-known cycle. The person loses control, abuses you, and then is instantly (usually) sorry. They even may go out, and buy you gifts including flowers. They will try very hard "to make it up to you". They may even try to be intimate with you. If you believe them, allow them to be intimate, even out of fear for further retribution, they feel all is forgiven. Everything will be "fine" for a short while until it happens again. It is sad but it is reality. You will easily begin to see a pattern of behavior.

I have some advice on involving the police. Through experience, it is not always best to call the police unless you are in dire physical danger. Nowadays, in most states, when there is a domestic violence call to the police, they will take in both parties. Unless there is obvious evidence; bruises or any other kind of physical damage, rather than argue, they take you both in. It then becomes your word against theirs if there is no physical evidence. This is where it becomes imperative to have some documentation, counseling, and help from an outside agency already going on. Many times your abusive partner has a plan on what to say or do if you call on the police. Recently, someone I know was reluctant to call the police. After repeated occurrences, it was advised they call the police. Their partner knew of this, started a fight, physically pushed this person, hit the record button on their phone, and taped this person reacting. All of a sudden the abuser got calm and quiet while they continued taping. The abused person was arrested for harassment. It is best to research and get advice from a shelter or another agency if there is no obvious physical evidence of abuse. I know all of this is hard to process, but there is unfortunately a "system" out there, and it is not always to protect the abused. Research, talk with the agencies available, and gain the knowledge so that you make wise and timely decisions.

Back many years ago, I called the police regularly but did not press charges. I just want to "scare" my ex-husband, thinking that he would stop abusing me. I did not understand what I was dealing with. I was also afraid that he would not make it to the jail, for racial reasons. Unfortunately, that issue still remains, but you cannot control this piece of the process. The most important thing is your safety and not getting wrongfully accused. Pray and with wisdom, think everything through. I am just trying to make you aware of some of the possibilities that happen nowadays.

If you decide to get a restraining order and are able to get one, do not in any circumstances break it. Do not let anyone convince you to go against it. You can put yourself into a dangerous situation. Use all the available help and maintain your distance and safety. Be very careful of your surroundings at all times. I am not trying to instill fear in you, I am trying to allow you to see all possibilities so that you can be wise and safe in your behavior.

Something else I want to address is if there are children in this relationship. Firstly, their safety is of the utmost importance. If you are being abused, do not leave the home without them. If you need medical attention or anything else that you cannot take with you, remove them from the home and place them safely with a loved one. It is not wise to leave them behind, even if your partner never hurt them in the past. Even if you are not leaving permanently, if your partner fears you will not be returning they could take it out on your children. Assure their safety first. It is very difficult during emotional times to think clearly, which is why a plan is necessary. Advice from a counselor or shelter is imperative.

Know when you leave and you are executing your plan, it is not over, Sometimes things might get worse before they get better. If you are separated, be careful in the surroundings that you allow visitation. If your partner insists on dropping by to see the children, do not allow this unless you have others with you. Unfortunately, it is during these times that your partner may try to hurt you again. It is also possible that they may use this time to force themselves on you sexually. There is something about once they can be with you intimately, they believe everything is fixed. If you have a restraining order, this hopefully will not be an issue. If you cannot get one, allow visitation only in a supervised situation. It is advisable also not to allow the other parent to take the children out of your home during this time. This is especially true if there are no official separation or divorce papers yet. Once there are official documents, you can call the police if the other parent has them when they are not supposed to and break the parenting time agreement. Again, I am not trying to make you fearful of everything, I am trying to enlarge your thinking and make you aware of possibilities. That is why it is always so important to pray to the Lord for wisdom and discernment daily. Many times after doing this, "my gut" has told me not to do something, and by listening to it I have averted a serious situation from developing. When we are going through draining and emotional drama, we definitely will not think clearly.

Once things evolve to divorce, it is a hard and sometimes a long process. I know that most lawyers cost money, and many times the persons who abused us seem to have family members who will pay a lot of money to "stick it to you". Many times the person abused and trying to leave the relationship does not have their own money or much money. Hopefully, there is legal assistance at your local shelter. By this time, if you have done your research and spoken to them, you will already have this information. It can seem such a daunting process to go through, but in the end, it will be a better life for you.

It is important throughout all of this process to be in counseling. If at any time during counseling, you don't feel supported, find another counselor. Counseling for your children is imperative also. Children tend to not understand when their parents break up, even if there is apparent physical abuse. Their cognitive development may not be at such a place where they don't understand that it isn't their fault. Even if they understand this, breaking up the family unit even for safety reasons, will be very difficult for them. Don't believe that you can help them or that they will be "OK". Just as you need to learn how to deal with your grief and find a new healthy normal, they do also. You are not the only one who needs to be healthy emotionally. You are an adult and many times have difficulty understanding how all this happened, how to leave, and how to become healed. They will have a harder time understanding and surely don't know how to navigate the grief and come to terms with the upheaval that has happened in their life.

Once the divorce process is over, there will be a long time of adjustment and grieving. Everyone grieves differently. Don't expect yourself to be "over it" in a certain amount of time. It can take a long time and you will certainly have your ups and down. Be kind to yourself, and treat yourself well daily. If you just need to take a bubble bath, a walk or a nap, remember to care for yourself. If you have children to care for, the best present you can give them is a parent that is calm and patient. I know this for sure, as I many times as a single parent I was not calm and patient. I now regret this, but it was a process for me to learn how to care for me.

I always put their care first and many times did not have the time or energy to focus on me. This is not healthy and is very exhausting. In that exhaustion, it is easy to lose patience. One of my counselors taught me in my years of counseling that we ALL have a little child inside of us.

How we treat that little child inside of us can affect our behaviors toward others. Since my childhood had so much abuse in it, my little child had a lot to learn and kindness to be shown to it. I had to understand and care for that child. I had to know that that little child in me would always be a part of me. Now that I was an adult, I could control what happened to her, and how to treat her. Sometimes during difficult processes that I have had to face, I had to be kind to her and care for her daily. It could be something simple like saying something positive to myself, taking a walk, or bubble bath. If I was not kind and caring to myself, I could not be a good mother. I finally learned this and tried very hard to do this, even though I was often exhausted. I also had to learn to be forgiving of myself. Through God's love, mercy, and forgiveness, I learned how to love, have mercy, and forgive myself. I believe that it is much harder to forgive myself than others.

Loving yourself is very hard to learn especially when you have been abused. When you are abused as a child, you learn a behavior that is "normal" to you. When you are taught that the reason you are being so severely punished is because you are bad, then that is what you believe. As the years go on, you do not realize this is what you feel. You think you are fine and have escaped the abuse, the rest of your life will be great. I thought once I escaped my home and my mother, that I had a lovely, wonderful life coming to me. After all, hadn't I earned it?

The main thing that comes from being abused as a child is low self-esteem and self-worth. Since I was taught I was abused as a child because I was a bad person, it stands to reason that I felt I deserved to be treated wrongly. When I married young, I was in love and saw no evidence through our courtship that my ex-husband was an abuser. It was three months into the marriage when he first hit me. I am saying this all to point out that when you come from this background, the first time as an adult that you are abused, you react differently than "normal". My normal was "I was bad so then I must be punished". The first time my ex-husband beat me, I asked what I had done wrong. If I had not come from that background, I believe my reaction would have been to leave right then, or definitely after time #2.

When I finally realized that counseling wasn't working and he was not serious about fixing this behavior, I then chose my safety and the safety of my child. I still didn't believe I deserved any better from him since it was the same learned behavior from my mother. She said she loved me too, just as he did. The thing that finally jump-started me into action was that my son who was 1.5 years old started reacting when his dad called my name in a certain threatening tone. My son would run crying into his room, climbing back into his crib to hide. I then realized if I wasn't smart enough to leave for me, I needed to protect him. I vowed when I left my childhood home that I would never again allow someone to abuse me or a child of mine. While I was not emotionally healthy enough to put a stop to the abuse myself, I could stop the abuse that my son was enduring by seeing his father beat his mother.

After a divorce, we have much grief and emotional healing to do. After my divorce, I did not realize this and thought the answer was to seek another man/partner. I did not realize that I was so emotionally damaged and far from healed. I wanted companionship and intimacy and many times mixed them up. Since I did not date much and married at 19 years old, I was very naive when it came to relationships. I believed a man when he said he wanted to be intimate with me because he loved me. I know this sounds pretty ridiculous but it is true. I was looking for a partner, long-term romance while they were looking for sexual relations. I for sure did not realize that what was intimacy with emotions for me was just plain sex for them. It took me a couple of years to realize that before I took a break from dating altogether.

I had children and while dating with children was difficult enough, it is not healthy to bring different men around your children. First and foremost, they are your first priority. While I did several times, take many years off from dating to focus on them, my education, and work, I am not telling you not to date until your children are grown and out of the house. I am just giving some advice from mine and other's experiences. If you want to date, do so away from your children. Get a sitter to go on a date. If you decide to date someone in a committed relationship, take at least 4-6 months before introducing them to your children. They have been through a lot of emotional turmoil already. If you wait that long, usually you can tell in 6 months if this person is worth your continued time and meeting your children. Then when they meet them, you can be sure that person will be around for some time. It is perfectly fine to do dating away from the home and to spare them a revolving door of men/women. Something else to be thinking about is, what you are modeling for them,(boys and girls). Girls will look to you to see how you are treated by men and your sons will look to you to teach them how to treat women.

Something that is very important before you can seriously think about getting into new relationships. There is a lot of healing and learning that needs to be done. Even if you did not see evidence of abuse before you married your ex, why did you stay? Is there something emotionally unhealthy about you that caused you to be attracted to that type of person, or to stay in that type of relationship? It took me many years to realize that we are attracted to something similar to what we are. If we are emotionally unhealthy due to our childhood or abused as an adult, we will attract emotionally unhealthy partners. This definitely has worked out to be true in my life. As I got emotionally healthier through counseling and praying, the type of men I attracted were healthier.

It is important in my mind to get counseling and to take time off from dating. I know that this is not a popular belief but you not only need time to grieve but to heal. I did not want to continue to live the same type of life or make the same mistakes. We are creatures of habit and it takes effort to break bad habits. Be good to yourself and take that time along with the counseling. Pray for the Lord to show you how He loves you. I know it is hard to understand how much He loves us exactly as we are, especially with our pasts. It takes time and studying the Word to understand just how much He does love us unconditionally.

It also takes time to get mentally and emotionally healthy so that we can finally, truly believe that we deserve the best. It is a lot of time and work, but the outcome is so much better than the alternative. If you spend years after your divorce going from one relationship to the other, and not doing the work necessary, you have wasted a lot of time. Usually, you will not find another person worthy of you until you believe your worth and what you so wonderfully deserve. I cannot stress this enough. For your children's and your well-being, give yourself the time to properly heal, grieve, grow, and forgive. You will then attract someone who will care and cherish you like you deserve. You will be ready to love yourself well and the Lord will bring someone who is supposed to care, protect, and cherish you.

We waste a lot of time and heartache settling because we are not ready. Yes, sometimes it takes a lot of time. I have been divorced for 44 years, and still believe that the Lord will bring that "one" in His timing. I will be totally transparent and honest as I have been in this book. I will admit He probably would have brought him to me sooner had I been ready. I was not ready. I did not understand what it took to be ready, to be emotionally healthy, and to love myself properly. I do not regret this though, because in all that I have lived and worked through, I am able to share it with other women. If I can help just one other person and save them from abuse, heartache, unforgiveness, and self-doubt, I will be very happy. Many years ago, the Lord told me He would use what I had gone through to help others. I consider this an honor and a privilege. It is very possible you will be used and called to do the same thing. I think it is amazing if we can use what has challenged us in our lives to help others. How wonderful to be able to "pay it forward". I pray that you pay heed to some of my advice and do not have as many years as a single parent, alone (not lonely) years and struggling through getting healthy as I did. I have always said that if my children or others could learn from my mistakes, all that has transpired is worth it. There are always reasons we go through things, even the very challenging things. Turn all things that have happened into some kind of good!

Chapter Thirteen
Dating After Divorce

While we will be focusing on dating after divorce, this advice and these guidelines are great for all dating experiences. To get back into the dating field after a divorce takes intentional steps. You need to find out what you want and what are deal-breakers (your boundaries). Also, what to look for and when is a good time to "put yourself " out there. It is a minefield at best, but here are some advice/guidelines for maneuvering it.

Divorce rates in America still run very high. Many of us, after years of waking up next to someone, will find ourselves alone. Along with the grief and healing from our divorce, work must be done on yourself. It is wise to take the time to grieve, heal, and always be open for the work that is going to be necessary to be emotionally healthy. Even if your partner did some egregious things, all the fault of a divorce does not usually lay with just one person. Find out what you contributed to the decay of the relationship and work on those things. It is very important not to step out too soon into the dating field. If you do, you will be dragging a lot of "baggage" into that relationship and lessening the probability that it will work out.

I know that now and then, someone will walk into your life within a short time of your separation. If that happens, continue to do the work and take that relationship very slowly. Work on staying in the friend zone until you feel emotionally healthy again and continue to improve on yourself. The quality of your relationship will be so much better in the long run.

When you leave a long-term relationship/marriage, your self-esteem takes a huge hit. The thought of dating again is extremely overwhelming. You can have a lot of self-doubt and believe that no one of good character will be truly interested in you. Many men are interested in sexual partners but not emotional partners. It is also very difficult to put yourself out there to be examined, judged, and rejected. You are coming back from a huge rejection (usually), and many times with your partner choosing another woman. As women, we are very sensitive and emotional creatures, so it is very difficult to feel comfortable dating again. It is easier to meet someone along the path doing life than, for example, using dating sites. Beware of online dating sites, because they can have so many distrustful people along with men playing a lot of games. Ask your friends that have been successful at meeting quality partners, what sites they use. Ask them what is best to reveal in a profile and what are some of the red flags to watch out for. There have been some successful relationships that have met on these sites. It is always best to pray as you are getting to know someone and take it very slowly. If you meet someone for the first time for a date, after much talking on the phone, never meet in a secluded spot. Don't let them pick you up; meet them at the destination and always let your friends know where you are at all times.

The first thing to do is to figure out our standards. What are we looking for? What are the things that are deal breakers for us? What are things that just won't work for us in a relationship? There will be no perfect partners out there. That does not mean we make excuses for shortcomings that in the end we will not be able to handle. A rule I like to use is that if 80% of a potential partner is good after getting to know them and 20% are things that are not so good but are not deal breakers, only then is a good one to invest some time with. Remember, it takes at least six months to get to know someone well. Many people put their best foot forward, but if they are faking anything, it will come to light soon enough.

The more that you have worked on yourself and become emotionally healthy, the more you will be able to expect from a partner. I suggest after a divorce, that you attend a Divorce Share group. It will go a very long way in getting over your grief and examining the factors that contributed to the divorce. You will have more to offer and of course, will want the same in return. Determine your ability to bring desirable traits to a relationship such as inner strength, kindness, intelligence, and affection to a relationship. I believe that if you are looking for certain character traits you should ask yourself if you have those traits. Realizing what you have to offer will also raise your self-esteem. If you think highly of yourself in a healthy way, you will want more from a relationship.

Another thing to assess and decide before going out there is what kind of relationship you are looking for. Are you looking for companionship only? Are you looking for a marriage partner? Are you looking for someone but not necessarily the "one"? It is important to assess this so that you know what you truly want. Depending on what you are seeking, your standards vary. You always will want a partner who is honest, kind, loyal, and trustworthy. If you are seeking a marriage partner, you will want one that is a good provider along with they will be focused on you and your needs. Are you that type of person at this time? Again, whatever qualities you are looking for, most of them you will need to exemplify yourself. If you want an emotionally healthy man, you need to be an emotionally healthy woman. A saying that has stuck with me my whole life is "What you are is what you will attract"! If you keep attracting men who are not healthy, ask yourself why.

It will be difficult to attract someone healthy, especially if you are coming out of an abusive marriage. Your standards will be skewed in the beginning because of what you have gone through. Your normal may not be a good and healthy normal due to being abused. That is another reason to work on you, finding a new normal and better standard. If you have worked to become that quality person, and have grieved and recovered from your divorce, you will attract a quality partner.

When you feel ready to date, here are five tips:

1. Develop a new support group. It is very natural to go to your friends who have been in your life for a long time for support. They know you well and care for you. Also, it is hard, but many old friendships that were friends with you and your ex will go away (as some should). They take his side, are unrealistic, and do not know the true details of what happened. New friends or a newer support group can help you adjust to your new life. They didn't know you back then and it can be refreshing to have new friends who know the new and improved you. Another benefit to a new support group, especially when being around those who are out there successfully dating and are emotionally healthy, it rubs off. It is important to be around those types of people that you are trying to become. Friendships are important because of the support, understanding, and time spent with your friends. Helping you to continue to recover while being positive in your new season is very important.

2. Assess your self-worth. If you are negative a lot of the time, you will attract negative people. The same is true of being positive. If you are a positive person, you will attract that. If you are a believer in Christ, and that is paramount of importance to you, you will seek someone similar. It is important if you are a believer to not only seek a believer but to make sure you are on the same page with your beliefs. Being "equally yoked" is spoken about in the Bible and is a key factor to a successful relationship. Start by making a list of your positive qualities. Share these with your support group and get their feedback. Ask them to be brutally honest so that you can see if there are any areas that they see differently. It is great to find out what you believe are your best qualities and to verify if that is what is coming across to those who know you well. Also, make a list of some affirmations that you would like to start claiming over your life. This can include positive scriptures and statements that you believe are where you want to be and how you want your life to successfully move forward. Again, focus on making yourself

better and taking care of yourself. When you learn to put yourself first and take good care of yourself, it will be easier to see that in someone else. It will also teach you how you want to be treated and recognize that in another person.

3. Work on planning some activities. You know the old saying, "he is not going to knock on your front door". You will not meet a prospective partner sitting on the couch. It will be exciting if you focus on the things you could not do before when you were with your ex. Make a list. Review that list and see what you can do with a friend or even by yourself. Most of the list you make will be things you can do without a partner, so go out and start doing them. You will meet people along the way with the same interests. That is a huge positive! During this time and until the right one comes into your life, be active. Remember your life is not on hold; life is for the living! Don't just exist! Even through the grief and recovery of the divorce, try to keep a few positive activities in your life. As you heal, the positive activities will grow and you will begin to enjoy your life. Don't be negative about your new season, embrace it and know that things will get better and restoration in many areas will occur.

4. Curb unhealthy cravings. During the grieving and recovery process, we will feel a lot of emotional pain. Cravings can develop that are self-destructive. Food is a big one and can lead to being more physically unhealthy. Those who do not like being single will jump into another relationship before they have done the proper healing and growing. We have beliefs that we cannot make it alone, especially if we have been in marriage for a good amount of time. Remember that when you get emotionally healthy, you will be stronger and enjoy times alone. If you can be a great person by yourself you will be a great part of a partnership when that time comes.

5. During this time you should have frequent contact with your support system. They can hold you accountable for unwise tendencies, spend time with you to keep you distracted and give

you that sounding board and companionship that is helpful. Do still spend plenty of time by yourself, working on yourself and getting comfortable with yourself. Explore all the exciting things that you have wanted to do for a long time. Keep a list of things that will successfully distract you and use this when you are starting to feel an unhealthy craving coming along

6. Prepare for pitfalls. The holidays, birthdays, and anniversaries are going to be very difficult. They will bring up good and bad memories for us. They will stir our deep feelings of loss and our loneliness more intensely. You will compare memories of your past and compare them to your current situation. Be careful not to isolate yourselves, especially during these times. Start new traditions and make small plans for yourself ahead of time so you don't think of your past so much. Participate in new activities with your support group so that you will not be in your memories and heartache. Ask your friends for help planning activities. It is healthier to plan so that we have something positive and fun to look forward to. (Psychology Today, online, January 2003, An Interview with Lisa Ling)

I am going to add a sixth tip that is very important if you have children. It brings a new perspective on dating if you have children. You not only have a possible partner affecting your life, but the lives of your children. It is very important to the well-being and emotions of your children to wait to bring that possible partner around them for a long time. You must first see what that person is truly about before introducing them to your children and affecting their lives. This is in the case of you looking for a marriage partner and that possible partner seems as if he would be a good husband/step-father. If you are looking for a companionship partner or sex partner, I strongly advise you not to introduce your children to them at all. Don't expose them to multiple people that are not there to stay. If you are seeking a marriage partner, you have been dating for at least 6 months, it seems as if the relationship is serious and will be long-term, then start to prepare them to meet that person. Six months is a good amount of time to get to know them better;

their character and whether it is a serious relationship. Introduce them slowly and introduce them as a friend first. I suggest no sleepovers with that person when your kids are with you for visitation. It just gets them confused and gives them possible false hope of a marriage. It also can cause problems with your ex-husband in the co-parenting arena. Use wisdom because our children don't have the maturity to process this all, they are children. Do not fall into the trap of thinking that they think like you or will understand things that you do, it simply is not the case. These are precious children that still have the minds of children and they look to us to protect them as much as possible.

In the end, re-entering the dating game can be fun but very scary. Establish if you're ready, your standards, your support group and do what is comfortable to you. Don't be driven by the emotion of loneliness. Make sure you are in the right frame of mind. Continue praying through each stage as you start to date. If you are looking for a life partner or marriage, ask God to walk with you through each step. Ask Him before the first date to direct you to the person you are to be with. After that first date, make sure to ask God if this is not the one you want me to be with, please remove him from my life. This will save you a whole lot of time and heartache.

You have learned yourself well during the grieving and recovery. Use your wisdom and always bounce things off of your support group. Try new things and be open to things you haven't tried before. When you are emotionally ready, it can be a wonderful adventure. Make the most of each step, live life for your best self, and keep in mind to enjoy the journey!

Chapter Fourteen
My Christian Walk

As was talked about in an earlier chapter, I grew up as a preacher's kid. We lived in the parsonage of the church...the home that the church owns. Dad did not make much of a salary, but living in the home that belonged to the church and was next to the church was part of his "wage."

Since we were the family of the minister along with the proximity of our home, it was expected that we were at the church non-stop. Whenever there was an activity at the church; square dancing, garage sale, kids events, women's meetings, etc. we were expected to be there and help out. It was a small church with maybe about 200-300 members. The whole 14 years that I was there – from ages 4 to 18 – when I left home, the membership stayed about the same, so there were not many people to help.

We were also expected to do things such as clean the bathrooms, the kitchen, and other parts of the church. We did have a janitor, but he could not handle all of it. I remember seeing a men's bathroom for the first time when I was about 9 years old. I was sent into it to clean it. I could not understand at that time why it was different from the bathroom I used, but I had to scrub it down. It was so gross!

Along with cleaning and assisting with activities at the church, it was certainly expected that we would attend every service that occurred in the sanctuary. As said earlier, all 6 of us children sang in the choir and played instruments of some kind. So there were many rehearsals involved in the times that we were next door at the church. So, we seemed to be at church all the time.

I remember that even though I was in youth group and Sunday school, I did not take my faith seriously. I did take my father (earthly) seriously and his position as a minister. Part of the reason that I acted this way I believe, was because I was always in survival mode from my mother's abuse. I focused on trying to stay sane in my mind and have some fun of one kind or another. I remember myself and a best friend, skipping Sunday school to just hang out with each other.

I could not really have her over my house because of my mother's behavior. Truthfully, I did not readily invite any of my friends to my home. My mother was unpredictable and would think nothing of berating me or doing some form of abuse to me even if my friends were there.

I remember one of my friends from school came over. We are still friends to this day and we still talk about that one visit sometimes. My mother chose to act out, of course, and I was so embarrassed. My friends did not believe that my mother could be as bad as I said she was. Well, suffice it to say, from that day forward, my friend did not doubt me. I never invited her over to my home again. If we ever wanted to hang out outside of school, I just went to her home.

One time, my best friend from church did come over Sunday after church. My mom went into a tirade and started yelling at me, telling me that we do not accept clothes from others. My friend's family had 6 kids like ourselves and had given us some clothes. I remember asking her why we could not accept them from that family but could buy clothes at the rummage sale. At least we knew where these clothes came from and the people who wore them. So my mother was yelling at me, standing at my bedroom door, meanwhile, my friend was hiding behind the door to my bedroom. My mother never found out she was there, but my friend was extremely frightened. She never questioned my stories about my mother from that day forward.

Another reason that I feel that I was not a more committed Christian was that our faith did not talk much about our "walk with the Lord". I did know in the Word, that we were not supposed to sleep with someone before marriage. It was not talked about much. Having a personal relationship with God was not discussed at all either, that I remember. It took many years and another church that I would become a member of in my early 30s, to understand and learn about all of these things.

I believed in right and wrong and knew the difference, most of the time. I went to church "religiously" until I was 18, and left for the military. After leaving for the military, a few weeks after my 18th birthday, I headed off to Basic Training at Ft McClellan in Mobile, Alabama. We were in Basic for about 8 weeks, and at no time were we allowed to leave the post nor did we have time to attend church.

I felt growing up, that since I was a Preacher's Kid, I was forced to go to church and to participate in all the activities that happened at the church. I was exercising my new freedom, to not go to church, and did not take my faith very seriously. I knew the difference between right and wrong and tried hard for the most part to do the right things and treat people the way I wanted to be treated.

After Basic Training, I went to Ft Ord and Ft Benjamin Harrison to do some military specialty training. It wasn't until I got to my permanent duty station that I had the time and was there long enough to go to church. A few days after arriving at my permanent duty station, I ended up in the hospital. I had been suffering from Mononucleosis for a few months. They did many tests, especially for my liver. It seems that Mono, especially having it for a while without treatment, can damage your liver. Thankfully, my liver was normal. The part of my body that did act up was my legs. I had tendonitis in my legs and it was very painful. Not only was it difficult to do much walking, running was impossible.

This was very hard to emotionally deal with, since up to this point I had been a huge athlete. I ran track in high school, along with playing volleyball and softball. I was very active and not being able to run hurt me physically and emotionally. I finally had to stop, take a break, and let my body heal itself. I remember thinking that I would be very grateful if I was going to be able to walk long distances again and especially to run.

I was involved with physical therapy during and after being discharged from the hospital. The Mono was gone, but the after-effects were not. It took months to slowly recover and get back to normal. I remember, of course, leaning on my faith at that time. I did not have a deep faith, but it was my foundation. I also remember talking with God about my illness and recovery. I asked the Lord if He would restore my body and energy. I might have even tried bargaining with him. I was 18 yrs at this time, and very immature in my faith. I may have been mature for my age- according to my High School teachers- but I was very immature in my beliefs of God.

I finally recovered and was able to play softball for the Army and do many sports later on. I continued to do my Personnel job at Ft Ord. Soon after returning there, I became engaged to Ed. Our engagement happened after about 3 months of falling in love. He left Ft Ben and was then stationed in Hawaii. We were married soon thereafter, on my 19th birthday. I applied for a Compassionate Reassignment to be there in Hawaii with him after we were married by my dad, back in New York. A few months after our marriage, I finally received my reassignment. I went to join Ed in Hawaii on the island of Oahu. He was stationed at Fitzsimons Army Medical Center and I was stationed at Fort Shafter, a few minutes down the road from the Medical Center. I was working as a Personnel clerk for a Military Intelligence unit.

Upon my arrival in Hawaii, we stayed with friends until we received our allowances for rent and food. Then we found our apartment. During that two-year stay in Hawaii, about three months into our marriage, he started to hit me. As discussed in the chapter, My Abusive Marriage, this went on for the two years we spent in Hawaii and the few following years we were consequently at Brooke Army Medical Center in San Antonio, Texas. Again, I was in survival mode. While praying often, I did not think about going to church.

When the hitting started, I felt – due to my abusive childhood- that I was at fault. I keep thinking I was not a good wife, and that I must have deserved it. Of course, we know even if I was a bad wife – which I felt I was not- I did not deserve to be beaten. I tried to be a "better" wife, but it was hard to be intimate with my husband due to our marriage falling apart. I visited a church a few times while in Hawaii. After the two years in Hawaii, we were both stationed in San Antonio, Texas. We moved there to attend job training schools.

Once there, things got much worse in our marriage. It was not until this time that I started seeking a church to attend. I am not sure how I found the Baptist church that I started attending. I was newly pregnant at the time and did not even know it. I felt very welcome at this church. It was very different from what I had grown up in, but I felt stirred and knew how much I needed the Lord. Sadly, the reality is that sometimes we don't seek God unless we are in some kind of serious circumstance.

I remember feeling that things were so hard and so unbelievable that I had to do something; I could not go on like this. Of course, when things are going well, we don't usually turn to God. He has to let the bottom fall out of our lives, at times, for us to "reach up to touch bottom." We have to be hurting something awful in some way to reach out to Him! During those times, God also places people in our lives to help us. He loves us so much that no matter what we do, He is full of grace and mercy, and helps us!

We had been married about 2.5 years when I started going to this Baptist church. I grew up in the Congregational faith but found a love for Gospel music from my friends in high school. So I purposely looked for a church that had that environment and music. It did not matter to me that I was one of the few Caucasians to attend this church. The "all White churches" had not impressed me along with most of my friends, from childhood on, were not White.

I befriended a wonderful woman at this church, named Mary. Her husband and she reached out to me, and many times invited me to their home for Sunday dinner after church service. We became close and she is the one who first told me that I may be pregnant. I shared with her that I thought I might be, and she felt my stomach and said she felt I was. I asked her why she said that and she said because it was hard at the bottom of my abdomen.

I found out very soon after that I was pregnant. I continued to go to this church and be friends with this family throughout my pregnancy. I shared with her, in private, some of the things that I was going through in my marriage. She did not judge but was there for me to talk to. She was older than myself, and really helped me to survive those few years. Not only did she help me through the pregnancy, but was there afterward.

I went on to give birth to my first child, Nathaniel at the young age of 22 years old. I know that I was young, but had been married for three years. I was ready, so I thought, to be a mom and this pregnancy was planned. I had always wanted to be a mom. I knew things were not going well in my marriage, but at this time I still had hope that possibly we could work these things out. Life was very hectic with me working full time in the Army, a new momma, and dealing with an abusive partner. I remember feeling such joy at being pregnant, giving birth, and being a mother. Even though I was going through hard circumstances at home, I felt peace when I was in church. I began to learn more about the Lord since I had limited knowledge from my youth. This was the beginning of my process to learn and mature in the Lord.

Mary and her family were there to help me emotionally and physically throughout the first year and a half of my first son's life. Things between me and my husband were getting worse. I knew that even though I did not believe in divorce, for our safety, I may end up having to divorce Ed. While in Hawaii, we did try counseling, but he did not seem serious about it. We did not try any when we were in San Antonio. Soon after my son's birth, some cheating was also beginning. I was beginning to hear stories about my husband being with other women and even possibly abusing them.

I think my breaking point was when one day, my son was about 1.5 years old, Ed yelled at me. His yelling was in a certain tone that conveyed danger to my son. He ran crying to his room and climbed into his crib. He was crying hard and I could not console him. Ed was screaming a lot and I was afraid he was going to hit our son. While his abuse was saved for me and he up until now had never hit our son, I was scared. I realized at that point, that if I could not leave for my safety and well-being, I had to leave for my son's. When leaving my childhood home, I promised myself, I would never put any child through what I had survived.

After a party at our home, and consequently walking in on him and a "friend" of mine, I kicked him out of the home. I was afraid of him, but so fed up with the abuse and now the cheating. I went into detail about what happened after this party, in the chapter talking about my marriage. This was the final straw. Ed lived outside the home for a few months. After getting some counseling and prayer, I told him that I was thinking of getting a divorce. I was afraid to get a divorce and also afraid to tell him I was even thinking of it. The day that we met on the base and I told him, he ended up hitting me again, busting my lip. I had to get our son from Daycare and called the police. That day started about 6 months into the process of divorce with him still abusing me and keeping me freaked out. I understand when women say they are too afraid to leave. I expected him to jump out of the bushes in front of our home one night, when I came home, to hurt me. It is difficult to leave an abusive spouse and a woman has to have a plan before leaving.

I continued to lean on God and my spiritual friends, to make it through. It was hard to maintain my calm for our son, so I stayed in prayer. Many bad things happened to me through that time, and through it all, I still loved him and wished it could be worked out. As each month went by and the divorce drew near, I knew that it would not work no matter what I wanted. I was in survival mode and protection mode for myself and our son. The only way I saw out of the stress, abuse, and constant fear was to leave him and to leave San Antonio.

The end of my second enlistment period was drawing near, so I decided to leave active duty and go into the Reserves while moving out of town. I ended up in the Denver metro area in Colorado. I did have some friends there and settled in rather quickly. I looked for a church soon after arriving there and tried for about the next two years. I remember thinking that I had to take good care of my son, and try to get my life "right".

I went to church off and on. I was working full-time the first year there, but then after that decided to go to school full-time. I was also in the Reserves. I met more wonderful friends, along with the ones I already knew, and they were instrumental in my survival. They helped me care for my son and consequent children during my Reserve weekends along with any time I needed them.

It took about 2 years to "remove myself from the dependency" on my ex. I dated off and on but focused mostly on my children, the Reserves, and occasionally, God. I felt that I was so naive…and I guess I truly was. I was married so young and did not know the "ins and outs" of the dating world. I truly believed that if a man slept with you, he cared about you. Yes, I know some of you are laughing…I know…how stupid.

I did not understand how after only 2-3 months, these men who said they cared, and seemed to care, took off. It was because they weren't looking for a relationship that had domestication in it…they were looking for fun and sex. It took me about 5 years of "being out there", to finally figure it out. By then, I had two more children, even though I tried to not become pregnant. I feel that no matter what the "mess" we are in, many times God blesses us anyway.

My children were all meant to be and were and are blessings to me. After, the third one was born, along with the drama I went through with his unfaithful father; I finally decided enough was enough. I decided it was time to get serious about God and stop dating and having sex. I needed to have my sole focus be on God first, my kids second, and providing for them third. Many times, I had to work 2-3 jobs to do this, but this is what I felt God wanted me to do and what I needed to do.

I want to say that after my third child, Chris was born, I returned to church. I was 32 years old. I was invited by a close friend that I worked with at Metro College in Denver. I was not used to non-denominational types of church. I experienced speaking in tongues, laying on of hands in ministry, and loud music. Also at this time, I was questioning whether God was real and why I felt no peace in my life. My life was full of struggle and survival. I asked God into my heart and rededicated my life to the Lord. I still did not trust Him. I asked Him to show himself to me. He did and has continued to do so for many years.

I started to feel peaceful during this time, even though there were day-to-day stresses of raising the kids alone. I started to see how He was meeting my daily needs and never leaving my side. The times I felt distant from the Lord were times I was the one responsible for the distance. I had so much to learn.

After about 5 years of this celibate lifestyle, I went out with someone who I thought was a Godly man. He was introduced to me by a coworker. She wanted to see if he could be a "big brother" to my eldest and I ended up dating him for a short while. During this time, I asked him not to start anything physical with me, because I wanted to stay celibate. One night, things got out of hand, and we had sex. I did not feel good about falling into that sin and consequently broke up with him. Approximately, 6 weeks later, I found out I was pregnant with my youngest son.

He was shocked of course, and offered to have "it taken care of", but I was not hearing of that. I had already done that a few times and at that time knew that those times in the past had been a mistake. This was certainly a baby, I had learned, and I was not going to compound our sin with another one, one of especially such magnitude. I did not know how I would make it with a fourth child, especially since raising three at that time was more than I could handle financially. I knew that this child was a blessing and meant to be. He had a purpose in this world, just the way his sister and brothers did.

I felt that the way I became pregnant, and also because I believe in God there are no mistakes…only ours, this child was truly meant to be. It was very difficult for me, due to being very involved in a new church that I was now a member of, along with singing in the praise team and leading the children's choir. How was I going to answer the question of "Sister Bobbi" being pregnant and not being married? It was very difficult.

The first thing that I had to do was to go to my pastor and his wife and make them aware of my situation. I first told my Pastor's wife and took a close friend with me to that meeting. I know she was in shock and did not know what to say. I explained the circumstances of the relationship. She said that she would discuss this with the Pastor and let me know what they would do. I was in leadership at this church and knew that even though the Pastor would support me, and my pregnancy, and not judge me, I might need to step down from leadership once the pregnancy started to show.

I know many people may say that this is a judgment of me but I disagree. I feel that even though the Bible says not to judge, the leadership of a church, and my "shepherd" must be discerning about the message that is put out from the pulpit by actions. The actions of the leadership must match with the words that are preached. I know that we all fall short and sin, but leadership needs to be as righteous and holy as possible. Many fall short because we are all human with a will of our own when we don't follow God's will. It is hard to do this and it takes a "dying of self" process every day. It is a process and a maturing in God has to take place.

I respect the fact, greatly, that my Pastor did not ask me to step down from my ministries, but instead asked as I started to show my pregnancy, for me to not be up on the platform. I asked a wonderful woman in the church to assist me, especially with the Children's Christmas Drama. She continued to assist me throughout the pregnancy and is still today, one of my dearest friends. She has been a mentor to me spiritually and many times in the following years, I looked up to her and her spiritual strength/faith. She was truly one of my spiritual mentors.

It was very difficult to keep attending church during my pregnancy. I know some people in the church judged me; I could see it in their eyes. What they did not know was that I judged myself more harshly than they ever could. I was stressed a lot during this pregnancy, but my friends and God helped me through it. The father was not around and would not be involved in my son's life until he was about 10 months old.

It was during this time, with me just becoming pregnant with my 4th child, my youngest, that God talked to me about my past. He said that He understood that I had been through a lot. Even though most of it was due to bad choices on my part, one day He would use ALL that I had endured and survived to help other women. I remember thinking that when He spoke that to me, all that I had been through would be worth it. I felt then and still feel to this day that if I could help just one woman; it would ease the pain and suffering. I know that all that I have been through makes me who I am today, but it makes it so much more bearable if it will help others.

I want to give honor to the church and ministry of Word of Life, now in Lone Tree, Colorado. I started attending this church When my 3rd child was 3 months old. I had all of my children dedicated and baptized at this church. Even though coon after starting there, I became pregnant as a single woman, this church supported me. Yes, I did suffer a lot of church hurt there, but the good outweighed the negative. Churches don't hurt you, misguided people do. Every time I would pray and ask the Lord if I could leave the church, He told me no. He knew that even though I would suffer some pain there, He planted me and my family there for a reason. I would raise all 4 of my children there, trying to give them the best spiritual background that I could. I would learn how to serve the Lord there through the many ministries I was involved in. I would learn how to enlarge my heart for others. I would learn so much about the Bible and how to walk in it. It was my church family for many years. I am very grateful to Pastors Tim and Gayla Bagwell for supporting me and my family well and for their ministry. It is a huge part of who I am today and whom I get to minister to today!

When the Lord spoke to me 14 years ago to start writing this book. I remember at the time asking Him when I would have the time to do so. I was in shock when He told me to write. I don't call myself a writer, even though I have written plenty of papers in college for my undergraduate and master's degrees. So, of course, I did not understand why He wanted me to write, since I was not a writer. Even though my last child had left home, I was still very busy working overtime at work, in church ministry, and with friends.

Soon after that, when my last child left for college, I moved to New York. I grew up there on Long Island and my mother was still living there. She has recently been diagnosed with Alzheimer's. I decided to move back there to try to help with her care. I had done the work in therapy for many years and had forgiven her for my abusive past. I wanted to continue to honor her as my mother and try to help her. I wanted to see if I could assist with healthcare, doctor visits and just be there for her.

So, I moved to New York to be closer to my mother. I know that many people cannot believe that I would uproot myself, after being gone from New York for 37 years, and move back there to help oversee my mother's care. This is especially hard to believe since she grossly abused us in all ways in our childhood, and many times through our adult years (emotional). I am a caregiver by nature. I was done raising my children after 30+ years and felt that I should be there to help my mom.

It takes forgiveness, of course. I will discuss that in a separate chapter since it is so important. God has asked me to have that be a separate chapter since it affects all parts of our lives. It was no easy feat to pack up the pieces of my belongings that I wanted to keep, give away the rest to friends in need, and drive 50 hours from Denver to Long Island, New York. I had a 12-foot trailer hitched to my small SUV along with my dog, and it was a long drive.

I left friends of 30+ years, my daughter, and my two granddaughters, to move out here by myself. I had planned to move back to Hawaii after all my kids were grown and out of the house. God had a different plan, and so that dream is on hold for now. I knew that eventually, I would move out here to oversee her care. I fought it, of course, because I am human and I knew it was going to be so emotionally hard. After her Alzheimer's was progressing, and I was spending a lot of time and money to keep coming back and forth to take her to the doctors along making sure she was not being neglected by her partner, I knew I had to finally make that move. Also, I did not have any choice but to try to get guardianship of her, since she was not being taken care of the way the family and her doctors felt she should be. I will talk more about this in my Alzheimer's chapter. I have learned a lot about the disease with all of this happening.

Once I started to write, I fully understood that this book cannot be written by my spirit, but by God's. I could not just sit down and write – I had to be "praised up and prayed up"! This had to be written by the Holy Spirit in me and under His direction. I also have learned even more about myself and about my relationship with God. I know that throughout the years, God has provided for me and my children. It was such a struggle, and hard to put it all on Him, but He did bring us all through. I learned that no matter how much He does for us, we still try to rely on ourselves and our own means. We never seem to learn the lesson that He will never leave us or forsake us and He will provide us with our daily bread if we just seek His righteousness and his kingdom first. The Lord had to heal me of pride and thinking I could do it all on my own. I did not like being superwoman but also did not like asking for help. That was very difficult for me. He taught me humility and that He would be my provider all these years. If it wasn't for Him and the friends he put in my life to help me, I don't think I would have survived all the challenges that were in my life.

I am continually learning that lesson. I had a sister out there in New York at that time that made this transition a bit easier, but she has her own family and full life. I was not able to see my mother every week as I would have preferred, but I saw her consistently and kept an eye on her well-being, safety, and health as much as I could. I tried to get Guardianship of her, but God did not want me to have Guardianship over her at that time. It was a blow, but I was determined to be there for her in any way I could.

In addition, I feel in my spirit that even though I initially moved her to be closer to my mother, God had additional plans for me. It was very difficult to leave my home church of 24 years, along with friends/family. Even though I have been through a lot with some members of that church, God planted me there many years ago, and never gave me the release to leave. I had to stay when I wanted to run away from the hurt that was directed at myself or one of my kids. I had to continually forgive people who hurt us, as God has continually forgiven me all these years of my shortfalls/sins.

My relationship with the Lord has grown and matured over these long years. He has always been there, no matter what, loving me unconditionally. He has not condemned me when I have deserved it, and as the Word says, death is the consequence of sin. He has continually forgiven me, as His death on the cross has given me. Even though I have known better, many times over, not to do certain things, I still did them. He loves me so much and has given me mercy and grace. He is the God of MANY chances…no matter how much and how hard we fail.

He has brought me through so much. He says He will not bring us around our challenges…but through them. We are not to stay in those challenges long, just long enough to rely on God and to learn what we are supposed to learn. I fully understand that over all these years all that has happened to me, both good and bad, makes me the person I am today.

God has used these things to grow me, mold me, and make me more compassionate. I cannot help those who have been abused or with any of the other challenges life has given me unless I have first been through them myself. I know that a lot of the hard times that I have been through, have been because of bad choices on my part. I also understand that since I had the childhood that I had, I made those choices out of misunderstandings and lack of knowledge. When I was in my twenties, I realized I could not control what happened to me in my childhood, but I had a say in what happened in my adult years. While it was a long process, and hugely through my heavenly Father's love, I can now see that He was there the whole time. If I had leaned on Him a bit more and trusted Him a bit more, I could have made a few better choices.

I want you all to understand that all things happen for a reason. There are lessons, growth, and understanding to be gained in all things. I will not regret the choices I have made or the reasons I made them, I will just move on to growth and learning. I try to not make the same mistakes over and over, but I still do. It has been hard to trust my Lord because trust has been an issue for me with my background. I never felt worthy of love due to my past, so it was especially hard to accept God's unconditional love for me. I only knew of conditional love…a love that was given under certain conditions or if I did certain things. He loves us no matter what!

Let me assure you, that even though He is so merciful and so full of grace, there are still consequences to "pay" for our wrong choices. The Word says that the wages of sin are death. God does not kill us but gives us many chances. Even so, He has to mete out some consequences, at times. If He did not, we would never learn. We should continually be grateful He does not make us pay our full consequences, and when He does give us consequences, is still there to help us through.

The road has been long and hard. It might have been a bit easier, had I listened, learned, and leaned on His understanding, not my own, much sooner. I am just grateful that no matter how long it took for me to do these things, He never left my side. He NEVER gives up on us, nor does he ever stop loving us. Even when we give up on Him or leave His side, He never leaves us. We surely can make our lives easier than we do, just trusting and leaning on Him at all times.

I am so grateful to God for all that He has brought me through and continues to bring me through. I am even grateful to him for the person He made me and what has happened to me. For instance, I always thought it was a "curse" to have a "big mouth" and to have a huge heart. I finally understand that He gave me my mouth for a reason. I usually joke that since my father was a minister and my mother a teacher I "earned it honestly". While this may be true, the reason He gave me my outgoing personality, verbal skills, and big heart is because these are the tools I needed to fulfill my calling.

He has specifically chosen me to be an encouragement to others and to walk in what He has called me to do. I am chosen for specific tasks and only I can fulfill those tasks. He equips me with what I need to complete them. What I had thought were bad traits of my character, He has shown them to be good and of Him. I remember a past Pastor saying about me that I "could talk the horns off of a bull". While I agree with him, I feel that the Lord gave me this heart, mouth, and compassion to help others.

God gave me a mouth to lift up Him and others. He gave me a mouth to help others. He also gave me ears to listen to others. It has been a many-year journey to learn to listen more and speak less. He gave us one mouth and two ears for a reason. It has taken me many years to pray before responding. Growing up in New York, that culture taught me quick responses and defense mechanisms. I had to unlearn many things. While my heart was very caring and giving, my exterior was quite rough around the edges.

As I have matured in life and through Christ, I have learned much. I have studied the Word a lot more. The Bible has basic lessons on how to live our lives. Even though our culture has greatly changed, the Word does not. God does not change. He is the same God now as He was back then. Miracles still happen! Once I rededicated my life to the Lord back in my early 30s, I have been seeking after God's righteousness. At times, I was not seeking very hard or working on my relationship with the Lord very deeply. That has changed as I have matured.

I realize now how much I need the Lord. I realize now how important it is to surrender ALL to Him. I am involved in different ministries now including missions. It is important to give to others and to care for others. All of us want to be loved, seen and valued. No matter where you live or how you live, we all have basic needs. I realize that now how we live is important. Not what we do as much as who we become. It has taken many years to be the person I am today. It has taken all of the trauma, victories, lessons and just hard-core living to be where I am today. I am grateful for it ALL! It made me who I am and allowed me to be more used to the Lord's benefit. I am honored to be chosen to write my story and to minister to those He has me ministering to. To ALL in my life, God be the Glory!

Chapter Fifteen
My Heritage

I have learned, as I have gotten older, that it is imperative to share our history with others. It does not take much to bring history into your family and to research your roots. I feel very strongly that I should share our heritage with the future generations. There is also a spiritual heritage as well and is just as important. I learned after many years in the church and under good teaching, that the generations after us will be exponentially more blessed and used by our Lord. I am happy to see that happening in my family with my children and believe it will come to pass with my grandchildren.

It has always been a dream/desire of mine to go back to the houses where I spent my years 0-4, before moving to Long Island. I was born in Waterbury, Connecticut while my dad was preaching at a church there. Then at the age of 2 years old until I was 4, (almost 5 years old), we lived in Pinepoint, Maine. That area is now known as Scarborough.

When I moved back to Long Island years ago, I realized this was the perfect opportunity to do this research. The first trip was to Woodbury. I didn't do any research prior, just decided on a spur of the moment to go to Connecticut. I went with a friend at the time who knew that area well. We left one morning and drove up to Connecticut and first found the hospital. It is now quite large and is very beautiful along with being in a beautiful setting. I took pictures of it and we continued on the road to follow the signs to Woodbury. As we drove into this small, quaint, and friendly town, we came onto Main Street. I saw a tall steeple in the short distance and asked my friend to continue to drive towards that steeple. I thought that it could not be the First Congregational church that I was looking for, since in my memory and history, most of the Congregational churches I know are not that tall or "large." Imagine my shock when we came upon the church, and it was indeed the First Congregational Church of Woodbury.

I was born there while my dad was the minister there from 1952-1957. I have no memories, of course, since I was an infant, but do have a very distant memory of visiting this area as a young girl around 6-8 years. old. We parked on the side of the church and I tried all the doors to see if I could get in. There was no one there, even in the office. I thought there would be since it was about 3 pm. Behind the church was a red barn that held a gift and antique shop. This area of the country is well known for its antique stores, but this shop had more trinkets and less furniture. I was instantly drawn to an antique doll with a long dress, parasol, hat, and a porcelain face. You twisted the doll and it played the song "Favorite Things." It was beautiful and sentimental and I immediately felt that I needed something to bring home from this place of my history. I purchased that doll along with some glass bowls and antique earrings. I also brought a necklace to give to my sister to commemorate this visit back in our history.

While talking with the woman working there, she let me know that she had the keys to gain entrance to the church, since she just happened to be a trustee in the church. I was amazed that God had put this together like this. I knew even further it was God because she told me that she was only in this store once per week. We walked over to the church and walked in. I was instantly in awe of its size and beauty along with the gorgeous stained glass windows that are normally in the congregational churches and churches of that time. I asked her if there were some records available that would confirm that this church was indeed the church that my dad was a minister of in those years. As we were walking down the hall to the front foyer of the church, she looked up at the walls. She was in front of me and asked me to continue into the front foyer. I came into it and looked up at the walls outside the sanctuary. Up on those walls I was shocked to find three large pieces of natural wood tablets, painted white in the front, with the names of all the past ministers had scripted on them. There he was - Reverend John P Cranston, Jr. listed for the years 1952-57. I just stood there and started to cry, feeling many emotions come over me. I was in awe that my search was very short but so fruitful. I was also wishing that Dad was here with me to share this with. The woman walked away for a bit and let me have my privacy. When I was able to finally compose myself, I took a picture of those tablets.

Once that was done I also took a few pictures inside the beautiful sanctuary. It reminded me strongly of the churches that were built in the early days when we came over from England. I had seen a church in Williamsburg, Virginia with the same style, architecture, and podium located up and to the side of the front of the church. Once I finished taking pictures of the sanctuary, spending a few minutes praying and talking to my heavenly Father and my dad in heaven, I walked outside the church to take pictures. I have pictures of the beautiful steeple and the sign which states that the church was founded in the late 1700s.

We walked back to the gift shop and I continued to ask her about the parsonage. I wanted to know about the house that I lived in from when I was a newborn until I was about 2 years old. She said there were two parsonages, one right next to the church, which was now a part of the gift/antique shop. The other one, the one that most likely was the one that we lived in, was down the street. I thanked her profusely and drove down to the house she said was the parsonage when we were there. I took pictures of that also along with speaking to a young man that was currently living there. He was a wealth of information and told me stories along with the history of the home. He was the maintenance person. the home for a very long time.

It was amazing to me that he knew all this information about things of the church/parsonage that took place so many years ago. It first occurred to me how important it is to pass this history down to our future generations because it is our heritage and our history. It is a part of the fabric of our lives and has a lot to do with who we are today. I took pictures of this residence and then took a drive through the small town to get the feel of it. While doing so, I had a flashback. I saw a famous inn/restaurant there that was still a restaurant. I looked at the driveway down to the side of the building, I remembered something from when I visited there as a young girl. I had a memory of us in that driveway, after we were all out of the car, the car brake was not on. The car started to roll due to the driveway being on an incline. My dad ran after the car and jumped into it, pushing on the brake. It scared me, both because I was worried about someone being hit by the runaway car and because I was worried about my dad being hurt. After that, we proceeded to the restaurant to eat our meal. I remember being upset about it for a while due to not understanding how something like a runaway car could happen at that age; and not understanding the mechanics of a vehicle.

    Funny, to this day I put on the emergency brake on my car. After driving around, my friend and I decided to start the drive back to Long Island. A few minutes outside of Woodbury, we pulled over and stopped at a small park we saw. It was pretty and at that time, even though I was not driving, I needed to just sit and reflect on the new information that I had just uncovered. I was so thankful to God that He led me to make that trip there. He opened the door for me to find out what I was searching for, and then I had finally done it. I was very overwhelmed by how it had turned out and very grateful.

    The next trip down memory lane was to research where I lived when I was little, from the ages of 2-4, before we moved to Long Island. That trip took me to Pinepoint, Maine. It is a small town 30 minutes south of Portland and it is on the coast. I had a bit more memories of this time, believe that or not. My sister and I had been talking about taking that trip for about a year or more, and finally, in 2014 we were able to go. It was again, a spur-of-the-moment decision. I had recently bought one of the few brand-new cars in my life and wanted to take a road trip. I was doing elderly care at the time and rarely had time off.

    We talked about it on a Monday afternoon and two days later, after an overnight shift, we left about 9:30a to drive from Long Island to Pine Point, Maine. This time, I had done a bit of preparation. I did not know the address of the house where we lived but had located the church. It was called Blue Point Congregational and was down the street from Scarborough, Maine. We left a note at the front door for them to call me on my cell when they returned home. We never did hear from them and we believe that they were away for a while. I called them last year near the holidays and let them know we were going to try to come in the following months.

It was a nice drive up to Maine, and we made a few stops. One of the stops was made at a rest area that had a gas station, restaurants, and some stores. At a Kiosk, I found some wonderful items from Yale University and Connecticut. Both my sister and I wanted a souvenir from Connecticut since that is where we were both born. I also found some wonderful items for my granddaughters for Christmas. Yes, I start shopping for Christmas, whenever I run across special items. I have also been known to ship boxes to them throughout the year, of clothes and presents. In addition, I found a few things for two of my sons' birthdays coming up in the next 2-3 months. I loved the things I found and consider them treasures because you cannot find them everywhere. It was part of the memories of the drive/trip up to Maine.

Once we arrived, I stopped by some old friends of my mother's and left them a note. We headed to our hotel next. We wanted to rest for a few and freshen up. After that, we decided to go and drive to see if we could find the house, and see the church on the way. So we drove about 10 minutes and soon arrived in Pinepoint, which is now part of Scarborough. We passed the church on Pine Point Rd and took some pictures on the outside. No one was there, so we couldn't get into it at that time. We had called the office of the church for a few days prior and that day, but were not able to reach anyone.

We passed the church and looked for Snow Road. I don't remember if my older sister had told me, mother's friends or it was in my memory, but Snow Road was the road I believed we lived on. We drove up and down the short road and finally, I stopped in front of a house that seemed to line up with the limited memories I had of the house. I started taking pictures of the house from all different directions. As I was finishing up taking pictures, a gentleman walked up to my car. He asked if he could help me and I told him that I believed that we lived there as small children. He proceeded to tell me he did not think so – I guessed we looked younger than we were. He asked our names and we told him we were two of Rev. Cranston's children. He said then that he thought we were right and that he was married to one of the Snows. I remember hearing about the large canning factory that the Snow's had which two of their products were Clam Chowder and Welsh Rarebit. He asked if we wanted to come in, and of course, we did.

We proceeded after parking in the driveway and met one of the Snow women, who turned out to have been one of our babysitters when we were very small. They had made changes to the house over the years but the fireplace was still there. We have a picture of all five of us kids (mom was pregnant with our youngest brother), and dad and mother. The fireplace had some added shelves but was the same. It was amazing to us. They explained some of the changes they had made and where the original steps, mud room, etc. were located. They even had a picture on the wall in a frame of the original house.

I was amazed to learn that her grandparents had originally lived in the home and when they died, left it to the church to be used as a parsonage. The last minister that had lived there had died there in the kitchen. They believe the house to be haunted. The house came up for sale from the church 10 yrs ago. after we had left there, in 1969. The granddaughter and her husband had decided to buy the home back to keep it in the family.

It was amazing to me that we had set out to find the house but found so much more. We were told stories about when we were little. Seems that my older two siblings had found a way to supplement their diet, which it has been told to us, was limited. I knew that my mother was extreme in her discipline (it is discussed in another chapter), but I never knew that sending us to bed without food for dinner was one of her forms of punishment. It was said that the cupboards were rarely filled with food and the church/community made sure we had nice Christmases with gifts of toys and food.

When they purchased the house, there were padlocks on the bedroom doors. We knew that when growing up in Bay Shore, Long Island, we had been locked into our rooms. The locks were the small "hook and eye" type. We had never known that there were actual padlocks on the doors of our rooms early on. Supposedly, they would lock us in and go out. My oldest sibling at the time was about 8 yrs. old. The locks did not surprise me but the severity of them did. Also, to hear that we had been left alone was shocking to me. Keep in mind that not much would surprise me about Mother, but I was surprised that Dad allowed this.

I can only imagine at that time the strain and deterioration of their marriage had begun. My mother had 6 kids in about 9 years, a huge feat for any person, let alone one who later on was known to have some mental illness. What those people felt, was at that time that my parents were very selfish and only worried about their image. They were out there trying to have some kind of social life with all these young children.

I have wondered why I have such a problem with claustrophobia. It also explains why I enjoy food so much and we have such a close relationship. Of course, there are heredity reasons why some people are heavier than others, but what food and how much you eat also play a part in your size and health. I was petite up until the age of 34 when I had my fourth and last child. My weight has never been low since and I have struggled since I was 34 to lose weight. The same thing did happen to my mother after having me, her fourth out of six.

While there, we also went to see the Portland Lighthouse. It was beautiful and there was a feeling of peace and calm in that beauty. We then traveled to downtown Portland to see where my grandmother lived for many years in an apartment. I do not know why I remember her address, but I did for all these years. She has been gone now for about 31 years. I remember visiting her apartment once as a young girl. It was beautiful and had many beautiful things in it, many of which my mother has had in her home all these years. Possibly, I remembered the address because back then, the only way to communicate with her was to write letters. We saw her once a year, for Christmas, as she would make that 6-7 hour drive every year to spend that holiday time with us. She would always say, I am at the crazy house and now looking back, I have to agree.

We were able to sit on the famous Old Orchard Beach and eat some great seafood, while on this trip down memory lane. Our last night there (we were only there for about 48 hrs.); we were going to go eat at an

Applebees near the hotel. I had a gift card that someone had given me for Mother's Day and wanted to use it. I then thought we were in Maine, where some of the best seafood in the US is located, so we needed to go eat some local food. We went back down near our old home and church to eat at a restaurant there.

As we were going by the church, we saw cars in the parking lot. I immediately turned in the lot and went inside the church. I heard people on the lower level, so I headed down there to ask permission to take pictures. They were in a meeting and I did not want to interrupt, so my sister and I just went upstairs into the sanctuary. It was beautiful, similar to the English churches as to the location of the pulpit, but struck me as "dark." I don't know if it was the feeling or spirit I felt or the gothic look of some of the iron-grated windows covering the organ.

I had been told that Mr. Snow had made that organ and that it was not played often nowadays. I took a few minutes to soak it all in after I took numerous pictures. We then hurried out to not disturb the meeting below. I was so in awe of the opportunity to get inside to take pictures to complete my family research into this period. This building had been built just prior to my Dad coming there as their minister in the late 1950s. The prior building was a white wooden building and was still standing, located just a few doors down. It has since been made into a beautiful residence.

On the way home back to Long Island, we drove through New Hampshire and stopped in Danville. Our old youth leader from the Bay Shore Congregational church when we were teens lived there. My sister has maintained contact with her all these years. She and her husband are still active, wonderfully kind, and warm people. We stayed about 4 hours with them, before heading back. We talked about Mother and Dad and what we learned. She shared a few memories as well.

I am happy that we finally took this trip. I fully realize that when you go back down memory lane and do family research, many times you will find out information that you would have been happy not to know. I believe in knowledge being power, even negative knowledge. It is better to have all the details and to paint the whole picture, to understand and analyze things. If you are missing a piece, then your analysis and knowledge forming could very easily be flawed.

In doing this family research, we have consistently also been trying to find my father's sisters. For some unknown reason, only supposing it was due to my mother and her paranoia, we only saw our aunts a few times. When Dad died, my sister contacted one of my aunts and she seemed not to be interested in meeting with us. We researched for a few years and finally, when we found them they had recently passed.

Another effect of my mother's paranoia and control over our family was that we did not find out that my father had another family before he married our mother. My Dad was married before and I have two half-brothers. I have never met them, but my sister has had dinner with one of them and his wife. I was a senior in high school when I learned of this other family. I am not sure whether my mother was jealous or thought it would make her look bad, she did not want us to know this information. I did know that she was 19 and my Dad was 32 when they got married. It would make sense that he would have had another family, to me.

Another piece of information about our family, my mother's, was only recently found out. We were told all of our lives that my mother was an only child. We recently found out that my mother had a brother. He was born three years before my mother and died the year before my mother was born. She was an only child, but I don't understand why we were never told about Wilfred. I was at her home recently and saw a picture of her and a young boy. Her caregiver said that my mother's boyfriend said it was my mother's brother, and that Mother told him she had a brother. Of course, that led us to start doing some digging and my sister found some information on Ancestry.com. The picture could not have been her and her brother since he was not alive when she was born. We tried to find out how he died, and so far have not been able to.

With all this research and history finding, we are now, at this age, wanting to know more. I know that my Dad had done his family tree, and showed it to me one time. I don't know what happened to that paperwork. I remember that on his side, all the men were named John or Jack. The first Cranstons to come over from England were on the Mayflower. A few generations later, a dad and a son were the Governors of Rhode Island. There is a town named after them; Cranston, RI and it is a good-sized town. I also remember that we were related to Lord

Stewart the VIII of England. I have done some work on my father's family tree and presently have traced the Cranstons (Cranstouns) back to the 1400s.

I now want to do our family tree, to include both my mother's and father's side of the family, to hand down to my children. When I put my father's name into Familysearch.org, I received many generations. When I put my mother's name in there, I only received about 5-6 generations. My mother's family is mainly German and must have come over as immigrants. I never remembered my Dad's parents since he was older and they had passed on. I remember meeting an aunt of my Dad's in a nursing home before she passed, she was 94 and had severe dementia.

It is important to gather this information, not only to fill in the blanks for you but to pass it down to your children, grandchildren, and great-grandchildren. Who came before, is a big part of who you are and who they are. I am going to work on putting together a family tree as far back as I can to give to my children and to be passed down. Nowadays, there are genetic tests that can be done to see what part of the world your ancestors came from. Also, you can find out relatives that you possibly didn't know about.

Another heritage to pass down to future generations is your spiritual heritage. It is important they know when you came to the Lord, the road that brought you there, the struggles, and the challenges. Everyone has a testimony and your family must know yours. In other chapters of this book, I have discussed my music and spiritual history/heritage. Your heritage helps your family understand the big picture about you and what you have successfully come through. These challenges that I have survived is the thread that makes up the quilt of my life, especially spiritually. It will give them a much better understanding and hope for themselves and their futures.

I will be including a few pictures of me in my childhood, my dad, these churches, and some of my children. These documents are part of my past and what makes me the person I am today. They are milestones and pieces of who I am. I suggest to everyone to do the research into your heritage as it is important to pass this down through the generations. It is an important part of the fiber of who we are.

Chapter Sixteen
Never Give Up Hope

As I look over the past 68 years of my life, I recognize one thing that has brought me through – my hope in God! Hope for a better future, my hope to make it through my challenges, my hope to see my kids grow into amazing adults, my hope to be able to continue to grow and learn till my very last breath, and my hope to share my life with its difficulties to help someone else. I firmly believe we are to continue to grow, get better, and do the very best we can until it is time to go "home".

My faith in God gave me the belief that these hopes and dreams would come true. Like everyone else, I had many things I wanted to see happen in my life. No matter what had happened in my past, I always had hope and faith that my future would be greater! I never gave up! That is so important because our trials and tribulations can make us want to give up. Sometimes life gets so difficult and it is hard to see our way through it.

A perfect example of this would be my children. I have written a separate chapter about them growing up and where they are today. The truth of the matter was the struggle was very hard, and long (30+ years), and seemed as if I wouldn't make it through. Now that I am on the "other side" of it all, I DID make it and I never gave up. They are doing well, no matter our struggles and now making better lives for themselves and their children. They are doing better than I am, exponentially, as they should be. That is what I was taught through the Word; that the generations to come will do exponentially better than us. I am pleased to see that in my family's life. I believe that my grandchildren will go on to make even bigger differences in the world and have larger talents/gifts.

The main thing is never to give up! When we are in struggles it seems so hard. We don't think that we are going to make it. We pray and lean on the Lord, believing that we will but we have our doubts. This is just being human. The difficulties make us tired and weak. We can't see our way through these hardships to see ourselves on the other end. The Lord says He will bring us through our challenges. Not over, around, under but through. We are not meant to stay in those challenges. We are meant to make it through them. I praise the Lord daily that I made it through. We have to believe that we will make it. We lean on God for his wisdom and direction to know how. We will make it through these challenges and we will grow in the process of it.

I believe that everything that happens in our lives happens for a reason. Now, it could be the reason that we just made a terrible mistake. So, what happens next is a consequence. Even so, I believe that God never leaves our sides, even in our messes. He meets us in our messes and will change things amidst all of it. There are always lessons and growth to be learned from all situations. So whether things happen that we directly caused, or happened to us due to someone else's behavior, there is something to be gained from it.

How we act and believe is the direct result of how we see our lives. Our perspective is very important. Which "glasses" will you put on to see your situation? Will you put on the glasses that always see what is missing and what you don't have? Will you put on the "glasses" that see what you have, how to best fix the situation, and still be grateful regardless?

Let's see if I can explain it better. Let's look at finances because that is something we all struggle through. We all need to pay the bills. We all need a place to live, food to eat, and clothes to wear. We all need the provision of our needs. We have wants, but the needs are the things we must have to survive. As a single mom for many years, there were not only my needs to be met, but those of my four children also. That was a much heavier burden for me because I would desire for their needs to be met before mine. I was responsible for them and they could not provide for themselves, so I needed to work to make sure I met their needs.

I am sure you can relate to me, many times I did not know where or how I was going to be able to provide all their needs. Due to there being 5 of us in the household, I needed extra bedrooms. In many places where we lived, I had to get very creative. I had to turn an open basement into a bedroom or two. We also moved often, sometimes every year. It was very difficult on the children, but necessary. I would find a great place that had reasonable rent. After the year's lease was up, they would raise the rent. To the tune of 100 dollars or more, and that was many years ago. There were times when we had to go to Food Banks. I was embarrassed at first, but my strong desire to provide for my children tampered with my embarrassment. There is help out there like WIC for babies, Food Stamps, heating help, and so on. If you work hard and do not make enough to get everything, do not feel embarrassed to reach out for assistance. I worked for 40+ years and many times more than one full-time job.

The Bible tells us that God is our provider. In the paragraph above, I believe that all the assistance we reached out for food and heat assistance was part of God's provision. I would knock on the doors of assistance and He would open them. It was one of the ways God provided for us. I never gave up because I learned through these experiences that no matter what it looked like, He was always going to provide for me and my children. He showed up repeatedly. When I was about to give up, something came from an unexpected place or person. I would be so grateful and know God showed up just in time, again.

Another example was after the children were gone. For many years, I have had trouble with my lower back. I believe it was never the best, even though I played sports for many years in school and in the Army. The sit-ups we were required to do in the Army were very difficult for me. Pushups were much easier for me. As I got into my 50s, after my kids were grown and out of the house, I started having more difficulties. Of course, I know that being the dad and mom for most of my kids and lifting many heavy items often, I was not helping it. When I was about

52, I started numbness in my hands when I got up in the morning. It was very bothersome, so I went to my doctor to have it checked out. I was at this time normally working 52-60 hours/week; this was my normal.

The doctor ran an MRI and found arthritis in my neck as the cause of my numbing hands. I had been injured by a patient during my days as a phlebotomist. I also had been in several car accidents where my neck and upper back had been injured. So as a consequence, arthritis sets in where those injuries first began. In the next few years, I had two very bad falls outside my job while on my breaks during my walks. During the second one, an MRI of my lower back was done, and two bulging discs were found there. I then went to physical therapy to try to strengthen the muscles around that area since without back surgery those discs would not correct themselves.

I continued to work around and through back problems for the next 4-5 years. When I was about 58 years old, things got worse. I started having severe pains and more serious numbing in my hands, more on the right side and went to see the VA doctors about it. More X-rays and MRIs were done. They found a herniated disc in my neck that was pressing on my spinal column. No surgery was recommended but I consequently went through about 1.5 years of physical therapy and acupuncture to manage the symptoms and pain. My back would spasm often and cause knots which caused great pain. I began to learn how to live with chronic pain.

It was very difficult for me because I was very active all my life and took care of 4 children and myself. I was now being given the challenge of trying to care for just me and it was difficult. I could no longer do any real work, so could not provide for myself. Sitting for more than 20-30 minutes at a time or standing for more than 10-15 minutes at a time, were no longer possible. Physically my body would not support what I needed to do to care for myself and provide financially. I was working about 60 hours per week caring for an elderly woman for the past 3 years when it all came to a head. She had just passed and I was unemployed and was looking for a job, then it felt like it all fell apart.

Keep in mind that I was a single mom of four for 30+ years, having some help from 2 of the children's dads, and I was used to working hard, long hours. I was used to being very active and taking care of 5 people well with God's never-ending help. Now, I could not even work to care for myself. Physically I was suffering but mentally I was devastated. I did not know how I was going to provide for myself. God had provided for me through my many jobs and hours. Now what?

It took me a long time to wrap my mind around the drastic change my life had taken. Since I could no longer work full time, I applied for disability. This sometimes, especially in a state as large as New York, can take about 3 years to obtain. It is a difficult situation at best. With no money coming in, how do you pay rent? How do you pay for a car payment? There are thankfully Food Stamps so I could at least eat. It became very difficult to find a place to live. I was faced with the strong possibility that I would end up in a shelter. I believed that God would make a way and that would not happen to me.

Being a Veteran I started asking around for any programs out there for the homeless or at risk of being homeless people. I knocked on many doors, again not giving up even though I was very discouraged and also, dealing with living life in daily pain. Even going to the store to shop for 15 minutes was painful for me. Through continuing to knock on those doors, I found a program. It is a government program through grants that helps Veterans to find housing, and pay a few utility bills along with helping to find employment (if you can work). I was so surprised and grateful. I had to wait a few months to start getting housing help, so I stayed with a friend's mom who graciously let me stay with her for 3 months. After that this agency paid my rent for 6 months and my deposit. The limit was low for the amount of rent allowed and difficult especially instead of the rental costs in New York.

They wanted me to stay in a rooming home and I knew that that would not work for me with my health issues. I asked if I could find my place, have it inspected by them, and then have the rent paid for by them. They said yes, so I went looking. As you can see, you can never give up and must continue to look/knock on those doors. God will open the ones that are meant for you. I was surprised to find a condo in which the owner was renting out a bedroom and bathroom, and the rent was cheaper than my allowable amount. I was excited. The agency went to inspect it and meet the owner. They were shocked at the quality of the place I found and pleased by the niceness of the person. God again showed up on my behalf. This was one of His provisions for me. I was approved and was able to stay there a few months past the time of my hearing for my disability. I was ecstatic!

My hearing came and was challenging too. Two weeks prior, my lawyer said he wanted to quit my case. We had been at it for a year. I had gotten my case expedited a bit because I was a Veteran. I also wrote a letter to my congressman and asked him to write to Social Security on my behalf. So, even though my lawyer wanted to quit and his belief that I had a 10% chance of getting it approved, I charged ahead. I serve a big God, and He moves many mountains. He had come through many times and I had faith that He would continue to do so. I did not give up even though it was looking very difficult.

The night before the hearing, I reviewed all of my notes and numbers that I knew the judge would ask of me. My lawyer had prepared me but there was one very important piece of my preparation that was not done yet. I went into prayer, also asking a whole group of prayer warriors to pray with me. I was specific in my prayers, asking God to give me peace, to give the Judge patience, to not look down on me unfavorably, and for her to see what was going on with my health. Yes, God answered all of those prayers. While I was very nervous, I trusted God to be with me and to help me.

Yes, God did answer my prayers. The judge was very patient, listened carefully even breaking into a smile, which they are not supposed to show emotion during the hearing. She gave me the whole allotted time for my hearing. When we came out of the hearing, my lawyer was very impressed with how well it went. I simply stated that God answers prayers. I was glad the hearing was over since we had been waiting a long time for it. I relaxed and told my lawyer that it was in God's hands. He still didn't believe that I had a good chance of being approved. He had said to me that I may have to start all over.

Normally it takes 6-8 weeks after your hearing to find out whether you are approved or denied. Again, God worked on my behalf and I got a call from my lawyer in a little over 3 weeks. He was talking to me very quietly and I could not hear him. I was very nervous since he felt I would not get approved. I had faith, and hope and never gave up. I asked God to move the mountain in front of me on my behalf. My lawyer said quietly I was approved for my disability. I asked him to repeat what he said because he was so quiet. He said you were approved and not only that, but everything we asked for we received. I fell to the floor (was in a store with a friend) and just started crying. I was going to be okay and God again was providing for me. He had once again answered my prayers and would be providing for me financially every month.

I am so grateful! Every time that check hits my bank once a month, I thank the Lord for his provision. Since I worked so much, many times 2 jobs, the amount that was paid into Social Security from all of my jobs was quite a bit. For this reason, my disability would be enough to make it if I was frugal. I could not continue to live in New York, because I could not live with others with my health challenges. For this reason, I left my beloved ocean and moved to Oklahoma. One of my sons lives here with his family and I was anxious to be near one of my children and my grandchildren. While I was not "excited" to move to Oklahoma, I felt led to do so. I have been here for almost 8 years. It was a hard adjustment, leaving friends in New York, as I had left my friends five years ago when I left Colorado. I can not believe how fast time flies. I am involved in many ministries here and God is continuing to use me mightily.

My son here in Oklahoma was involved in a new church, a church plant from a nearby large church. The church was small, not the type of worship I was used to, nor was the music the type I was used to singing. The congregation was mostly in their 20s and 30s, with maybe 2 people at that time around my age. The church we had been members and very involved with in Colorado was large, with different races and financial "levels" along with the music being more what I was used to. We were involved with that church family for over 25 years, with my children being raised there. I say all of this to show you that I was totally out of my comfort zone. I was moving to an area that I did not particularly care for but I would be around one of my children with my grandchildren. I attended my son's church for a few Sundays with my son and his family. My son and his wife were the leaders of the worship band and very active in assisting the pastor in starting this church plant just 6 months prior.

My son was convinced I would choose another church in OKC to be a member of and get rooted into. I expected that also. While I did check into other churches, God told me to plant myself in this one. He constantly takes me out of my comfort zone, but my goal first and foremost was to do His will and to be used by Him. So, even though this was so different and uncomfortable in the beginning, I stepped out into God's will. God used me mightily for the 2 years I was there. Unforeseen circumstances had me searching for another church. I visited a church that some of my single momma friends were attending. I loved it! I was looking for a church that was rooted in the Word, knew about and sought the Holy Spirit, was non-judgemental, and had members of all ages. I have been at New Song for about 7 years now.

I am leading a senior ministry that God gave me a vision for. I am also leading a single moms group that is growing quickly. When I first started getting planted at New Song we had just a few single moms. We were involved in a single-mom ministry non-profit in the community called REAL. Now because our church is growing so rapidly, more single moms have started attending. Now we have a strong need for this group. These moms need to feel community and know they are not alone in this journey.

I am also doing one of my favorite things, worshiping with the Worship Team. I am still growing as a musician and a Christian. I expect to continue to grow until God takes me home to be with Him. I have been singing since I was a little girl and music has a special place in my heart and my family. Another area in which I serve is Outreach. We go on mission trips, both domestically and internationally. We also work in our community. I have been volunteering with a Christian hospice doing administrative work in the office and visiting patients. I am now on staff part-time. My desire in all that I do now is that it involves ministry and giving back!

It has been so amazing to continually be used by the Lord in all of these areas. Now I will be honest and tell you at times, I miss my friends in different states and my beloved ocean. What keeps me going is my hope, faith, and being used by the Lord. It is the most important thing for me. He is using me to change lives, which has been my lifelong dream. If I can help just one person, my life is fulfilling. While I work to help others, my hurts and disappointments seem small. There are always many more who are worse off than you and struggling. I learned throughout all these years that especially when I am hurting and going through a challenge, reach out to help someone else. It puts your situation into perspective and you can always help others.

This whole world and even the part of it that is our circle of influence is our missionary field. Even when you are traveling, standing in line at the store, you will meet people that they will minister to you or you to them. Let us go back to what I said in the first paragraph of this chapter; it is all about which "glasses" you choose to wear. It is all about how you see the situations you find yourself in. I am going to be very transparent, as I have been throughout this book. When I was going through the disability process, I was depressed. I was very uncomfortable not being able to control my finances, my place of abode, and all the other problems that went along with it. It was a long process, with no quick fix. It took constantly being on my knees, praying, to make it though. Yes, God had some lessons in that trial also.

I became closer to the Lord through the fact everything was out of my hands. I like to make a home wherever I live, and being in the constantly changing and unstable environments was challenging for me. It was a struggle that caused me much worry and anxiety. I even lost a car in the process and in the end, had to file bankruptcy. I also had to find a new home for my beloved dog and lost most of my material possessions such as furniture and other household belongings. When I moved to Oklahoma, I had all that I still owned in my used car along with two large boxes of clothes sent ahead to my son's house. No matter what the struggles were, the most important thing to remember is, I made it. God sustained me through all my difficult times. I now like to call these trials adventures. At 60 I was moving to a new state and starting over again. I chose to put on the glasses of adventure.

I lost many things going through the disability process and earlier in my life of single parenthood. No matter what, I did not give up. I always had faith and hope no matter how hard it got. I chose to look at my surroundings and to point out what I had, instead of what I didn't have. While this is not easy, it is a learned outlook on life that I have to this day. I am so grateful that God has provided for me through my check that comes once a month and many other ways. I am grateful that though I live in pain, almost daily, I have much to be thankful for. Until the Lord heals my body, I will continue to wake up each morning thanking him for what I have. I will live around my pain, constantly reaching out to others to make their lives better. I will continue hoping that all that God has spoken over my life will come to pass.

Some things happen in our lives that look like a problem or a distraction from our goals. It might just be that they are still God's provision and lessons. So try to stay positive, and continue to have hope and faith that all things will work out for good for those who love the Lord. Take one day at a time; do not worry about tomorrow's problems. I wasted a lot of time worrying when I was raising my children. I now have learned that I manage what I have control over and the rest I no longer worry about. In all things though, give them to God. I had trouble for many years surrendering my ALL to the Lord. I would put some things on the altar for God to handle and then pick them back up again. The Lord says to leave it all at His feet. Believe in Him for all things. When you spend time worrying about things in the future you waste your "today." Be grateful for each day, praying for your daily bread and God will continue to provide. Sometimes it is in ways that we don't know of or look different than we would expect.

Just do all things for the Lord in the spirit of excellence and you will be provided for. There will be times when your "baskets" will be overflowing with God's blessings. In these times and even in times of lack, reach out to help others. Many wish they had it "as bad as you do" for their situations are so much worse. You can always find someone else who is worse off than us. Continue to look at what you have, not what you don't. I know it isn't always easy, but I am still trying to be patient for a few dreams that haven't been fulfilled. When God appears to be saying no, He is saying wait for something better. He knows the plans He has for us. They are great plans, prosperous plans, and supernatural plans. They are bigger and better than we can imagine. He sees our future and knows so much more than we do, so trust Him. Continue to be grateful and content with all He has blessed you with and know that He isn't done. Listen to His will, act on His leading, and continue to be used by Him. Seek first the Kingdom of God and His righteousness; He will add all the other things to your lives.

Lastly, continue to study His word and pray. Studying the Word will continue to give you hope and faith. Storing the Word in your heart makes sure that when those hard times come, you have scripture to get you through. The Lord is the same today as He was in the past. He is still in the miracle-working business! He is still performing miracles, so believe. Never give up and continue to be grateful. If you look at what you have instead of what you don't, you will remain positive and thankful. Continue to share with yourself and treat every situation of every day as a new opportunity to learn something. We can also possibly teach something new to someone else. Every situation's lesson is something that is needed to learn to handle the situations coming in our future. God is always equipping us for those things He is calling us to do. The tools are given to us when we need them. Look around, how can you be used today for the Lord? Live life expectantly and watch and see what He has in store for you. No matter what hardships you are going through, know that they are temporary and they will pass. What "glasses" are you wearing? Leave it all to the Lord and give Him your best!

Chapter Seventeen
My Children Today

My greatest honor from God was to become a mother and raise my four children. I became a mom at the young age of 22. I know I wanted to be a mom but did not realize how unprepared I was to be one. I was in an abusive marriage and on active duty in the Army. I was dealing with a lot. I would say being a mom was the highlight of my days even though I was ill-equipped. As discussed in an earlier chapter, I had a very abusive mother. She was physically, emotionally, and mentally abusive. Needless to say, I did not have a very good role model from my mother. I would find out later in life, just before my dad passed away, that mom very possibly had a Schizophrenic/Paranoia disorder.

Looking back as a mother, I have regrets. I know we all do but I like to be transparent and honest. Due to many reasons mentioned in earlier chapters, I did not have a lot of patience. I lived in a state of extreme stress and worry. I had four children and had to work 60 hrs per week for most of my adult life. While these may sound like excuses, they are facts. I look back and wish with all my heart that I was so much more patient and did not yell so much. I feel bad that I did not use more kind words and take time to listen more to my kids. I am a much better grandmother than I was a mother because I have learned from my mistakes. I also have learned to walk closer to the Lord and have allowed Him to change my heart (me). Regardless of my past shortcomings, my children are amazing!

I want to start with my firstborn, Nathaniel. In Hebrew, his name means gift of God. From the moment he was born till now at 46 years old, he continues to be that gift to me and our family. He was a very bright spot from my abusive marriage that ended in divorce. Both his dad and I truly were excited about him coming, as he was a planned pregnancy. From the time that he was six months old, sitting in my lap, he was moving to the beat and trying to sing. He was memorizing Michael Jackson tunes, including the words at the age of two.

I would like to tell you a funny story from when Nathan was little. He got upset with me one time, and at this time he was the only child in the family. I have been a single mother since he was two. He was about five at this time, and he decided he wanted to run away from home. Of course, inside of me, I was freaking out! I was trying to teach him a lesson that it's a scary world out there! So he packed a little suitcase and he started out the door with me watching where he was going. I was afraid to let him out of my sight. A couple of minutes later he came back and said he needed something to sleep on, so I gave him a little pad that I rolled up. I let him leave again, keeping my eyes on him. He came back again, walking around the house, and asked where he was supposed to go. I told him that I didn't know but maybe you should think about that. Since he was still a little mad at me, he walked out and walked around our house and the next-door neighbor's house. Then he comes back again, knocks on the door, and proceeds to ask me what's for dinner. I said spaghetti, he said "Can I run away after I eat?? It was both scary inside and funny at the same time.

I guess I should've known that he was going to be a very independent child since he was the oldest. He helped me as a single parent immensely. At a young age, he asked if he could help me in the house. Later on, he would be asked to watch the other kids, if I had to run out for something. As he aged into his teenage years, we all knew that he was very gifted in music. He competed year after year in youth ministry competitions and won every year. Unfortunately, it was very frustrating to his peers. One year there was a severe snowstorm and the competition was about an hour away. There were blizzard conditions, and very little traffic going from where we lived down to the competition. I had a family van and

I was willing to drive them down since I was used to driving in a lot of snow. Colorado has many whiteout storms, so I asked our pastor if it was ok to drive the kids down. He said the church van was not going to go, but if I wanted to, I could go down there. Before leaving, I had to call all of the kid's parents to get their permission. We started down the drive. We got about 20 to 30 minutes in white-out conditions, and Nathaniel told me that he needed to go to the bathroom. I asked if he could hold it because if he got out of the car I would lose sight of him. I wasn't sure he'd find his way back, but he was complaining of his stomach hurting badly. I pulled over slowly and let him out and kept the window down a little bit. I kept calling his name so he could find his way back to the car. He finally made his way back to the car.

We were just following other cars, hoping we would not end up in a ditch. We arrived at the competition after driving for two hours with 30 minutes to spare. When we walked into the room where the competition was I could hear all the sighs. I felt bad for the other kids, but this was his last competition before he would go off to college, so I wanted to make sure he made it. He sang a solo and he also sang a duet with one of his church friends, Chantel. The good part about the drive was once we drove an hour we were out of the white-out conditions, and when we got down to Colorado Springs, it was fairly clear that it was just one of the many adventures that I have had with Nathan.

Nathan was also a very smart child and in fourth grade, he was moved to a private school on scholarship. He did very well in school scholastically but did have some problems adjusting to the private school culture. The ethnicity of the kids at the school was mostly white with very few black children. Nathan was a multi-racial child. He was multi-racial at a time when it was not very popular; he was born in 1977. They had just changed the law I believe in 1972, that you could marry someone outside of your race. I got married to his dad in 1974, so the culture was not very tolerant or accepting of multi-racial marriages, let alone children. I described my father in a previous chapter. He was someone who saw good and bad in everyone regardless of race. He saw character instead of skin color and taught me to feel the same. I had friends growing up of all different races.

Nathan went to private school from fourth grade all the way to senior in high school. He did very well in school. He worked very hard and he got an academic scholarship to Stanford University. He spent four years with a Bachelor's and a Master's there. After that, he went on to do paralegal work. He thought at that time, he wanted to become a lawyer. After working in the field for a while, he decided not to. He would go on to get more education with a Master's in sociology and start working on his Doctorate in Sociology/Racial Studies. He did not finish his doctorate, but he went on to later get a Master's in Business Administration at Denver University.

I want to let you know that Nathan is a very intelligent man. He has struggled with depression and anxiety. Some of it is biological and some may be the struggles in the time he grew up. Not only is Nathan a bi-racial child, but he is also gay. He was moody as a teenager, but I believed it to be just a normal teenage thing. Later I would find out that he was struggling with other issues. I am so proud of the man he has become. He is very talented and highly educated. At times it is hard to find quality work because he is overqualified. He does not give up. We have had some struggles in his adult life with times that we did not talk. I felt strongly that if you are upset with me, we should talk but at no time did I allow any of my children to disrespect me. That is all in the past, of which I am relieved.

I highly respect him because he stays true to himself and like his mom, is very honest. He has an amazing heart and is a very caring person. I am very grateful he was my oldest and helped me so much. Many times I had to work long hours and I would bring the kids with me while they all worked on their homework, but he would have to babysit. Also, he helped me maintain the house and do housework. He was a very good cleaner, he understood what clean was according to my standards. He continued to help me until he went away to college. It was a big adjustment to have him leave our household.

Lastly, I want to add that it took two days for him to enter the world. He came in with a large head, which held all those brains of his but tore his poor mama. The first time the nursery worker handed him to me to feed him I was questioning whether that was my child. He says let me see your name then it says read the child's name and also says read, so why are you questioning? I said because his hair is straight, I know I can be a little crazy at times. I accepted him and fed him and from then on he was called Punkin until he got into school. Nathan was truly meant to be the oldest and fulfilled that role amazingly.

Carrie was the next one to be born. She was born in May just five months short of Nathan's six-year birthday. She may have been a surprise but I was eagerly looking forward to her birth. When I found out she was a girl, I was very excited. My best friend at that time was my Lamaze coach. We eagerly prepared for her birth. It was very exciting to buy little girls clothes and have a shower for her. The day that I went into labor, I walked around a lot. I didn't want to be put in bed. I was in active labor for a while before I finally lay down in bed. It took her eight hours from start to finish to appear. She was a beautiful, straight-haired, olive-skinned beauty. She also ended up being very independent, very fun, and enjoyed life. Carrie was born between the junior and senior years of my first Bachelor's degree and I was 28 years old. She went to college with me during her first months of life. In the summer I had two self-paced courses so I took her with me. When she woke up, I fed her and when she went back to sleep, I went back to work on my schoolwork. Nathan helped out whenever he could so I could study. I was only in school at the time so I had plenty of time to spend with both of them.

As Carrie got older, I learned that she was going to be what Dr. Dobson has labeled a rebellious child. If the sky was blue, Carrie would try to convince you it was black. It made for some very interesting back-and-forth between us. I think some of it was her exerting her independence and not trying to fit anybody's expectations. After all, she was the second child and sometimes I believe that they don't feel seen. I'm sad to say that we had a lot of fights when she was a teenager and she seemed to always be grounded because she was always in trouble. I wish it wasn't like that. She was always a very social being with a very caring heart. She didn't like school much but loved being around her friends.

I always felt that Carrie didn't like that she came from a single-mom family. Most of her friends in high school had two-parent homes and I believe she felt like she was missing out. Our finances, or lack thereof, affected her also. She felt strongly that because most of her friends had two parents, they had more in the way of materialistic things. She was never a "material girl", but maybe would have liked to see less struggle financially in our home.

Now I enjoy her so much and since she is a mother now, I think she understands how hard it can be, especially as a single mother. She has two wonderful girls now 13 and 16. They are my oldest grandchildren. They live in Colorado and I get to see them for Christmas and in the summertime. I wish I could spend more time with them; they are growing so fast. She is a very caring and loving mom. She has a lot more patience than I did when I was a mom. I enjoy my grandgirls very much and they're very smart, beautiful, kind, and caring.

Unfortunately, Carrie also struggled in a marriage, which was abusive at times. She's a single mom like I was a single mom. She has been divorced for about 10 years and it has been a hard road for her. It's a very difficult way to raise children, but she has many friends and family who are there for her. I try to be whenever I can. She has also struggled with lots of grief in her life. Many of her friends have died and she also lost her fiance about 4 years ago to suicide. She is working her way through a lot of trauma also. She is an awesome survivor!

Carrie is 40 now. She remains a very caring and giving person. We had a rough time when she was a teenager but I'm very grateful that as we both have grown older and wiser, we have walked through forgiveness along with grace. Carrie is a very important part of my life as are all of my children. I want to add that Carrie's father disappeared from our lives when I was pregnant with her. When I told him I thought I might be pregnant, he disappeared. I later found out that he already had 5 children and that he was still married. We found out later in life after he passed, that he had many children. Carrie has been able to be in contact with her half-sisters and her grandmother on her dad's side. Carrie is a very family-oriented person, so I am glad that her brother Nathan researched for her some information on her dad. This gave her some closure, as I am sure she always felt the sting of not having a dad present when she was growing up. I was fortunate to have close friends who had great husbands who served as role models for her.

My next child's name is Christopher. He was born when I was 31. He grew up behind Carrie. It might have deterred him from being much of a problem child, since Carrie and I were always at odds. By the time Chris was in preschool at the age of two, we could see that he had athletic abilities. There was a big wooden board leaning up against the wall of the preschool that had holes cut out. The teachers would have the kids throw bean bags into the holes. His classmates were throwing them on the ceiling and all over the wall; very rarely getting them into any of the holes. Chris was nailing them straight into many of the holes. His teachers let me know his eye-hand coordination was exceptional. They felt that he was probably going to be a natural athlete that did not pan out to be true.

He was also very energetic. He had a hard time sitting down. At one point, the teachers at the charter school thought he may have ADHD. I had him tested and he was negative. I learned to speak with the teacher each year and let them know that he is a kinetic learner; he learns on the move if you allow him to get up and pass out papers, go to the office, or do something mobile during the day, he would be better behaved. He will learn and do better in class. Because he had so much energy, I put him in peewee football at the age of seven. He loved it and he was very good at it. IT allowed him to use up some of that excess energy. It also taught him how to be part of a team, and how to work together with other kids and other adults.

He went on to play football up until his last year of high school. He had scouts from different colleges looking at him, but in his senior decided to not play football. He wanted to work at the bank instead so that he could get himself a car. He went off to college at Oral Roberts University and got a Bachelor's in Business. Chris was also musically talented; singing and playing instruments. With the help of a friend when he was in high school, he taught himself how to play the guitar. He started writing music at that time. I was shocked as I had always thought that he was going to be going to college on a football scholarship. He chose to go to a Christian college and get his Bachelor's in Business. Instead, he was very focused and he did four years of college in three years. While in college he taught himself how to play the piano. Today he writes music, sings, plays the piano, and plays the guitar. It ministers to this mama's heart when he does praise and worship and is involved in his music. Right now he is not doing that, but hopefully, he will find the time to return to music.

He went on to use his business degree to work in the bank, and at the age of 25 he was a branch manager of a bank in Oklahoma City. He later went on to work in commercial real estate. He was very successful there and still does investment deals today. He is 37 now and co-owns a bath and kitchen remodeling company. He recently was a VP of commercial loans. He is a gifted businessman and is currently my financial advisor. He is married with two children, 7 and 11. I can see these grandchildren for 1-2 days every week. I pick them up from school and take care of them until he or his wife gets home from work. I am blessed to spend time with my grandchildren here regularly.

I want to mention that Chris is a very caring, very patient, and very giving person. I would say his love language is a gift. He is very kind and thoughtful. He watches out for me since I live here. As I get older, sometimes I stress him out but he shows mercy and grace and patience. He recently helped me buy a home and I'm afraid I put him through his paces. I call him my financial advisor as he helps me make financial decisions and manage my money. It is very helpful to have the business wisdom that he has to influence my life positively.

His dad was involved in his life very little. I'm sad to say that it affected Chris a bit in his early adult years but now he is an amazing father. He did not have a role model to lean on, but he learned quickly. I am very grateful for him in my life and for his watching out for me. Of course, he is a jokester and is always "pulling my chain." He is very funny, and caring and we enjoy life here in Oklahoma together!

My fourth and last child, Jonathan was born when I was 34 in 1990. As I look over the years I'd like to feel that he was the glue that brought the rest of them together. He was the perfect last installment into our family. He also is quite the character. He has an amazing sense of humor and is very active and musically inclined. He's very thoughtful, intellectual, and downright hilarious. I'm afraid by the time he came along, I was raising four children by myself mostly, and I was very busy.

His dad was in his life and saw him frequently. He would see him every other weekend and a couple of weeks in the summer. He would take him on vacation so they could have their family reunion together. He grew up with close relationships on my side of the family, and his dad's side of the family. I am grateful that his father was involved in his life. The other kids ribbed him a lot, but he would always come back and tell them, "At least, my dad's in my life!" Ouch! It was the truth, though sadly, he was the only parent that was involved with their child. It wasn't always easy, but it was nice to know that I had some support from him. Jonathan went on to play peewee football also and started about the age of eight. He went on to run track in high school and played football. He did the short distances in the high hurdles. It was funny to always get the question about whether his dad ran track or not because he was very talented. I would laugh and say no. I was the one that ran track in high school. I was a sprinter and I ran the short hurdles. It was a lot of fun in his last years to go to the track meets and even to the state track meet. He did very well and it was very exciting to watch. He went on to run track for Oral Roberts University, graduating with a theology degree (four-year, local pastor). After he got out of college, he went on to work at a boarding school for at-risk kids. It was a Christian organization in which he was a counselor and then a regional Director. He loved the work. He was working with the children and trying to figure out what was going to work for them. They had been kicked out of regular schools and had to be sent away to get help. They stayed there for a year. Many times, the kids would go back to regular schools and back to their families. He enjoyed the work and was successful after working there for several years. He later decided to move to Austin Texas. He did several different jobs and eventually started substitute teaching after being there for a few years. He took an interest in learning English as a second language And for the last 56 1/2 years, he has been living in China. Jon has been teaching young children, high school-age, and college-age students. He has been enjoying himself traveling, teaching, and Cajun cooking. He sells his food and always sells out. He wants to own his restaurant one day soon.

  God's tremendous gift to me was my four beautiful, intelligent, and caring children. My greatest honor is to be called their mom. It was a very hard struggle to do this almost alone for 30+ years, but it was so worth it all. When we did have time together, I liked to take them to parks and events outdoors so they could get fresh air and great exercise. I felt that even though we struggled, we were a close family. I kept them in church because I felt at that time it would keep them out of trouble. Plus, I wanted to instill in them, basic biblical principles of how to live a good life and how to be a good person. As every parent looks back, they wish they did things differently. Hindsight is 20/20 after all. Even though I have some regrets, I felt that I gave my all and did the best with what I had.

My kids have taught me many things; they have taught me to love unconditionally like I never knew. I knew the love of my father, but I also knew the abuse of my mother. I tried hard to not be like my mother and then to look at other mothers, to see what the proper role model was to be for my kids. I did have help from many friends along the way including my Lord. I'm very grateful God was always walking by my side, even if I felt like He wasn't there. I know now He was there.

I'm very proud of my kids and all the hard work they have put into their lives. I'm a proud grandmother of six grandkids, five girls and one boy. Their age range is five years to 16 years old. It is so awesome to see their different personalities. It also amazes me to see ones that are very similar to their parents. I also think it is interesting that some of my grandkids look more like me than my kids do. I guess when they say it skips a true generation. I pray over my children and my grandkids every day. Our world is very ugly and very evil. I ask God to protect them, to allow them to continue to be good people and good citizens. I'm very proud of my children and truly enjoy getting together with them and spending time with them. They give me a hard time, so I just let them talk and laugh. I thoroughly enjoy their presence and our times all together.

Being a mom will always be my greatest treasure in my life. I've learned that though life will have many challenges and many difficult times, God will bring us through those times. We become stronger, smarter, and wiser through the challenges. Once we survive those challenges, we can help others along those similar paths. Life is a journey and an adventure. So much to be learned and so much to have along the way. Whatever path you choose to live your life on, try to live it fully by being the best you can be. Don't ever compare yourself to anyone else. God made us uniquely and has called us to our own individual purpose. Live a thankful and grateful life! The Lord has brought you through and given us so much.

Chapter Eighteen
Where My Life is Now

I HAVE BEEN WORKING ON THIS BOOK FOR APPROXIMATELY 14 YEARS. I have walked through many things in those 14 years. God has brought me through a process of healing, learning, and growing. I am a firm believer that until I take my last breath and go to heaven, I am to continue to grow into the best person I can be. The callings that we have in our lives don't end when we become a "senior.". We continue to walk in them, grow in them, and be led by the Lord.

The sins of my past have been taken away. I have atonement for them when Jesus died on the cross. I have asked forgiveness for sins known and unknown. He has thrown these sins as far as the East is from the West. "Go and sin no more" is a lifelong process of walking in relationship with the Lord and allowing our hearts to be transformed.

Over these 14 years I have been working on this book, I have learned much about myself. I have taken the time and the space to grow, to mature, and try to understand things that have happened in my past. I have learned that through much trauma and life's challenges, our circumstances do not define who we are. They are temporary even if they last a while. They are things to get through with God's help and to overcome. They teach us many lessons.

I have been back to therapy recently to deal with PTSD due to military sexual trauma and relational trauma. I had forgotten a lot;

stuffing most of it deep down in the busyness of me raising my children. When I hit my 60s and (I slowed down in life), not working so much, it started to surface. Even though I have learned many coping techniques through being a single mom and being a manager in telecom, I still had more to learn. For this reason, I went back to counseling. Now as I look over my life, I can understand why my patience was shorter than I would have liked, and why I was so easily triggered in many circumstances. I understand why I lost my cool very quickly with the stress of being a single mom of 4 children. I understand now why I was so easy to trigger in many circumstances. I have learned why I reacted in the ways I did.

I have allowed God to mature me and grow me, as I have continued to strengthen my relationship with Him. I have been serving in the church for many years, mostly in women's ministries. At this time, I lead a Single Moms group and recently started the Seniors Ministry. I also sing on the Worship Team, am a greeter along with being a volunteer for missions work in our community and in other countries. I have learned a lot through all the different challenges I have survived, and I want to help others walk through these same traumas, especially women. God told me about 30 to 35 years ago, that all the trauma that I went through as a child and in my early adult years, he would use to help other women. I have been walking on that path and I believe this is one of the reasons that He asked me to write this book.

It was not an easy book to write, and I always prayed and asked the Holy Spirit to be with me as I wrote each chapter. I would not end the book and publish it until God told me it was time. I've had many of my friends say "When are you gonna get that book done?" When God says it's done, it will be done. As I look back now, I think that the chapter on sexual trauma is an important chapter to put in the book. Not until I went back to counseling and dealt with some of the sexual trauma that I experienced in the military and my early 20s, could I write that chapter. In addition, within the last two years, my spiritual life has changed quite a bit. I never dreamed I would be where I am spiritually today. I had to learn who Bobbi was. My identity had been a mother for many years. It was in these last 14 years or so, I learned who I was and how I got to where I am now.

I want to give glory and honor to God for how we have overcome together the challenges that I had to walk through. He equipped me to do so; He knew I was going to have to go through them. He knew what was gonna happen in my life before I did, so He gave me special qualities inside of me that would help me survive all the challenges I would endure. I have always wanted to give back, and I love serving the Lord. I love being used by Him and consider it an honor to serve Him. I love the Lord and I love the joy in my heart because of Him. I love the blessings that He has given me and the favor that He has shown me throughout my life. Even when there were struggles, there were positive things that I could focus on to get through everything.

He sent people my way and ministry to help me and teach me how to be a better person. Here is where I want to honor and show appreciation for the life-long friends He has blessed me with. One such friend had been with me for 57+ years. We became friends when we were seven. We remained friends throughout our childhood and through many of the years of my being a single parent. I know that she is one of the main reasons I made it through that season of my life. We were there for each other through the difficult times and the joys. We raised our children together. We spent many birthdays and holidays together. She helped me tremendously through the years I was in the Reserves and needed someone to stay with my children when I went away for two weeks in the summers. I will be forever grateful for her and her husband's presence in my life and the lives of my children.

Another lifelong friend and I have been friends for 40+ years. We also raised our children together and were there for each other through thick and thin. We both have walked through some horrific things, but we were always there for each other. She remains one of my dearest and closest friends today. I see her yearly in Florida and we spend time enjoying one of our greatest shared passions; the beach. She is an amazing mother, cook, and buddy. We always laugh hard and long when we are together. There is much mercy and grace for each other and we are helping each other down this road called being young-minded seniors. We are living our best lives now and still supporting each other along the way.

Another friend of mine has been a friend for 40+ years and we also have walked many challenges in life together. She is a prayer warrior and has taught me much about the Lord and the Word. We see each other 2 times per year when I go home to Colorado. She is always there to listen, to pray, and to encourage me and my family! She is a caregiver also and even though she walks a hard path at times, is always uplifting and positive. I believe we encourage each other and keep each other grounded in the Lord.

The last close friendship I want to mention has been in my life for over 30 years. We also raised our children together. This couple has seen many hardships but always has been my mentor. I have seen God operate so many times in their marriage and in their children's lives. They are my brother and sister; in Christ and life. They are truly "family". They accept me for who I am and who I am in the process of growing to be. We all have been growing and have been an important support network for each other during all these years. They have taught me much spiritually especially through them being Messianic Jews. We met at Word of Life years ago and became friends when our youngest sons were a year or so old. Our sons are now 32 and 33. They have helped me with my path as a single mom, especially with all of my moves.

I cannot sufficiently articulate what these and other friends have meant to me in my life. I have 3 very good friends in New York that I don't get to see very often. They are also the type of friends that when you do catch up, we just pick up where we left off. All of these friends have helped me to walk this crazy path called life. I know that they were part of the "Army" that God supplied so that I could have assistance. He provided them for me. Our friendships grew because we were honest and transparent with each other. We told each other the truth whether we wanted to hear it or not; in love. I learned that to have a good friendship you have to be a good friend. They helped teach me what being a good friend means and how to do it. I will be forever grateful for their hearts and time in my life so that I do not have to walk this path alone. I love them from the depths of my heart.

Recently I fulfilled a lifelong dream to go to Bible College. It has been 28 years since I finished my Master's Degree in Organizational

Management. Since then I have always desired to go to Bible College. I was not able to do so financially. In April 2022, I found Christian Leaders College online. They are accredited and their classes are free. You can take them with the Institute side for just a certificate - like continuing education. On the College side, they are free but you will pay some administration fees. When I signed up in April 2022, the admin fees were 3K for a Bachelor's degree. I received a 1K discount for being a Veteran. They have the Bethesda Pool Scholarship and after applying, I was approved for another 1K off. So my total cost for my Bachelor's Degree was 1K. When I was about to pay off the debt of 1K and was finishing my Bachelor's degree, they had a sale. They were offering 25% off of my remaining balance. So the Bachelor's Degree I received cost me $750. I was so blessed and honored that I was able to return and fulfill this lifelong dream.

The reason I am going into finances is so that others can realize their dreams for a small amount of funds. I set out to get a Bachelor's in Christian Leadership. I have been a leader in the work world and wanted to extend my knowledge. I also wanted to do an emphasis in the area of Women's Ministry since I have been involved in this area for decades. There are opportunities to also be licensed and ordained in different areas through the Christian Leaders Alliance. This is all online schooling done at your own pace. It took me a year to complete my Bachelor's with an additional emphasis. I did not transfer any credits from my previous degrees because it had been so many years and I wanted to get all of the knowledge offered now. It was a lot of work and hours per day, but it was finally done. I graduated in April 2023. If you have a desire or a dream, do your research, and don't give up!

I learned a lot about Christian history, the Bible, leadership, and the different roles in today's church. Halfway through, God gave me a vision for a Seniors Ministry at my church. We have since gotten approval and started this important ministry in September 2023. In addition, through this process, the Lord directed me to get my Minister's license and ordained as a pastor. He had a different plan than I did when I started this schooling.

Our church is rapidly growing and for the most part, the membership is 20s, 30s, and 40s. As the membership grows, so does the senior population. I felt the need for them to have their separate ministry. I have done some elderly care in the past along with taking care of my mom who had Alzheimer's. Being a senior myself, now at the age of 68, I see how much our society does not value seniors. Seniors like anyone else need to be seen, heard, and valued. We all need community so the new senior ministry at our church, called OASIS (which stands for older adults still in service) strives to build community. We focus on what I like to call the three "Kingdom C's": Connection, Community, and Callings. I have another woman and one of the husbands on my leadership team. Our mission is to build community within this age group and to give back from all the wisdom we have learned.

We do many fun things while God continues to download visions and ideas. We are growing in community and outreach. I believe that down the road a bit that God may have me visiting other churches to help them start up a similar ministry for their Seniors.

Currently, we have our coffee on the second Saturday morning and game night once a month. We have special interest meetings with our first one being on women's safety quarterly. In addition, in the fall and spring quarter, we are doing day trips. In November, we went on the Heartland Flyer train from Oklahoma City to Fort Worth for the day. We did some sightseeing down there. We had a very good barbecue and saw a Water Park downtown. We then came home to OKC. It was a long day, but it was fun and a great opportunity to get to know each other. Other areas that we are interested in developing are hospital/shut-in visiting teams for our seniors. We are also interested in some of our senior men discipling younger men in the church. It sure has been fun doing all of the different events and getting to know everyone. The best part of this is building a community where everyone feels seen, heard, valued, and needed. We exchange ideas and see where in our church we can be used.

I am also leading a single mom group at church. We have more and more coming into membership at our church, and I want to give back from my many years of experience. I am very excited about what

God has in the future for me in ministry; I am his willing servant and constantly want to get back to others.

I have been involved in mission work in Mexico for the last two years and am looking forward to doing another trip this year. One of my main goals is to build God's kingdom community and to serve others. I love going into different cultures, learning about them, and just listening. I have a friend who is an international student whom I met through a community ministry and she just graduated from college with her master's. I was honored to walk with her as she was new to this country. God gave us to each other, and I am blessed by her relationship and presence in my life

My goal has been for the last few years to be in ministry 24/7. I see that goal coming to fruition with the ministries I'm involved with along with my current Hospice work. I look forward to more ministry and continuing to serve Him. I love the Lord with all my heart, and I especially love how He leads me, guides me, and uses me. I seek to go deeper in my knowledge of His Word and to walk with Him closer every day. I firmly believe that without Him, I wouldn't be where I am today. I would still be caught up with all my challenges, and all my trauma, and I wouldn't be able to be healed. I also wouldn't be able to give back because I would not be healed properly. Healed wisdom and discernment is very important in serving God and I ask for it daily. Every day I desire to be the light of God shining through me that shows others the love that He has for them. He loves us unconditionally, no matter what mess we get ourselves in, or how we choose to do the wrong things. He still loves us, and he still blesses us. Just like my four children. They are all blessings even if they didn't come in the best of circumstances. God continues to bless us even when we're messing up. He forgives us and He shows us much mercy, grace, and love. We can continue to show the same for our neighbors, family members, and friends. The greatest commission that was given to us from Him, is to love others, as we love ourselves and to love our God, with all our hearts. We are to go out and grow His kingdom and show others His love.

Another dream of many years was to again own my own home. When I moved to Oklahoma originally 8 years ago, I did not believe I would be here long. I wanted to move back to Hawaii after living there in my early 20s. That was not God's plan though. Last year, I decided since I was going to be here for a while, I should buy a home. I had wanted to in the last few years, but I was not in a financial place to do so. I needed to pay off some debt. Once I did that last summer, I was ready to begin looking. The Lord has blessed me with my own home. I am very excited to do more ministry here in my home. I have been working very hard on the inside to update the property with the help of my brother and my contractor friend. Now I am working on the outside. It is an avenue that God is using to fulfill the dreams of the things I have always wanted to have in my home. It has been 15 years since I owned my last property! I am excited to use my home for ministry and to love others well.

I embrace His will, direction, and wisdom. I look forward to continuing to grow, learn, and walk in His will and with His leading. I am His servant in whatever He wants me to do and however, He wants it done. He has spoken over my life many times and I thought I knew what that would look like when it came to pass. Be prepared for it to look very different than what you think. No matter, it will be beautiful as God answers His promises and uses you to give back to others. Remember to remain humble, willing, and above all else, to always give GOD THE GLORY!

www.ingramcontent.com/pod-product-compliance
Lightning Source LLC
Chambersburg PA
CBHW070057080526
44586CB00013B/1089